THE LITTLE BOOK OF

monsters
and creatures

THE LITTLE BOOK OF

monsters
and creatures

FIONA GOBLE, SUSIE JOHNS AND ZOË HALSTEAD

NEW
HOLLAND

First published 2013 by
New Holland Publishers Pty Ltd
London • Sydney • Cape Town • Auckland

Garfield House 86–88 Edgware Road London W2 2EA United Kingdom
Wembley Square First Floor Solan Road Gardens Cape Town 8001 South Africa
1/66 Gibbes Street Chatswood NSW 2067 Australia
218 Lake Road Northcote Auckland New Zealand

www.newhollandpublishers.com

ISBN 9781780094458

Managing Director: Fiona Schultz
Publisher: Lliane Clarke
Designer: Lorena Susak
Photographs: Mark Winwood and Shona Wood
Production director: Olga Dementiev
Printer: Toppan Leefung Printing Ltd (China)

10 9 8 7 6 5 4 3 2 1

Keep up with New Holland Publishers on Facebook http://www.facebook.

Contents

Sewing

Introduction

If you want to stitch yourself a troupe of quirky new friends, then this chapter contains all you need to inspire your stitched creations. The cute creatures in this collection are made from easy-to-sew fleece fabric, as well as from fun felt and recycled socks and gloves. Fleece is available in a wide range of colours, though you could recycle old fleece jumpers into bright and colourful appealing monsters, if you like.

There are three small-scale projects to make in the Three Mini-Monsters - Wilf, Melvin and Prudence – they're little enough to be made quickly and easily, and large enough to make a significant impression on a little person. These monsters would make fabulous gifts too, and not just for a child. The strange shapes make them delightfully appealing, and the soft fabric means that they are soft, squishy and above all cuddly. You could make a whole host of characters – all with different personalities

We've given you plenty of ideas here for body colours and facial expressions and if you're feeling creative, you could personalise your creatures, giving them hilarious or grizzly expressions as the whim takes you. So, sit back, take a look through this chapter and choose your favourites. Have fun.

Tools and Materials

TOOLS

Before you start making these fleecie monsters and stitched creatures you will need to check out your sewing box and general supplies for some basic equipment and tools. You are bound to have some of the items you need already but there may be some things you will need to borrow or buy.

PHOTOCOPIER OR COMPUTER WITH SCANNER AND PRINTER, PLUS A SUPPLY OF THICK PAPER OR THIN CARD AND SOME STICKY TAPE.

The templates provided are shown actual size. The easiest and most accurate way to transfer the templates is to photocopy them onto thin card stock or thick paper. Alternatively, you can scan them into your computer then print them out. In some cases the templates have been split over two pages; simply join at the dotted lines and tape together.

SEWING MACHINE AND
SEWING MACHINE NEEDLES

You can easily sew these monsters and their accessories by hand but a sewing machine will make the task much quicker. A machine that does zig zag stitch is useful for some of the monsters but one that simply does running stitch will also be fine. Your machine should be fitted with a needle suitable for medium-weight fabrics. A standard European size 70 or 80 (US 11 or 12) needle is ideal. It's a good idea to have a few available as machine needles can bend or become blunt quite easily and you may need to replace them fairly often.

NEEDLES FOR HAND SEWING

You will need two types of hand sewing needles to make the monsters – a standard sewing needle and an embroidery needle.

You will need a standard sewing needle (a 'sharp') if you are hand sewing your monsters and accessories. Even if you are sewing by machine you will need this type of needle for closing the openings used for stuffing, attaching some of the arms and legs and sewing some of the monsters' features. You will need an embroidery or crewel needle for stitching some of

the monsters' facial features. This type of
needle is a sharp, medium-length needle that
has an eye large enough to accommodate
embroidery thread.

IRON
You will need an iron when making some of the
monsters and their clothes, to press open seams
and to fix bonding (fusible) web and appliqués.

WATER-SOLUBLE PEN OR QUILTER'S PENCIL
You will need a water-soluble pen or quilter's
pencil to draw around the templates and to mark
some of the monsters' features before you sew
them. They work like ordinary felt-tipped pens
or pencils but the marks are easily removed by
spraying or dabbing with water. The pens usually
come in bright blue and are the best option for
marking light and medium-coloured fabrics.
For darker fabrics, choose one of the pencils,
which are available in a range of light colours,
including white and yellow. These pens and
pencils are widely available in craft and
haberdashery shops, and through mail order
and internet companies that supply accessories
for patchwork and quilting.

ORDINARY PENCIL
You will need a pencil for tracing some of the
appliqué shapes onto the backing paper of
your bonding web. A pencil is sometimes
also useful for pushing the toy filling into the
monsters' limbs.

SCISSORS
Ordinary scissors are fine for cutting your
template card or paper but a pair of good quality
sewing scissors are essential for cutting fabric.
You will also need some sharp embroidery
scissors for cutting out small items such as
the felt eyes featured in some of the projects.
Make sure that you keep your sewing and
embroidery scissors strictly for cutting fabric
and threads as using them on card or paper will
quickly blunt them.

DRESSMAKING PINS
You will need a small number of dressmaking
pins to hold your work together before basting or
sewing. It's a good idea to use pins with coloured
glass ends as they are easier to see and less
likely to get left in your work by mistake.

TAPE MEASURE
This will be useful for checking the size of your fabric pieces before beginning your project.

PIECE OF FINE COTTON
To protect your work, you will need a piece of fine cotton, such as a handkerchief, when ironing the appliqués in position.

SAFETY PIN
You will need a small safety pin to thread the elastic through the casing of some of the monsters' clothes.

STITCH RIPPER AND TWEEZERS
These tools will come in handy if you make a mistake and need to undo your work. A stitch ripper has a point on the end and a sharp blade and will enable you to undo stitching without the risk of cutting or pulling the fabric. They are widely available in craft and haberdashery shops. Tweezers are useful for picking out any cut stitches that remain in your work.

MATERIALS
All the materials you need to make the monsters are available in dress fabric shops and haberdashery stores or from mail order and internet companies. The main fabric used for the creatures is polyester fleece – sometimes called 'polar fleece'. This is the fabric used to make items such as fleece tops, hats and scarves. Some creatures are made of felt and knitted socks and gloves. You will also need polyester toy filling to stuff your monsters and small quantities of felt and embroidery threads for their features. Depending on which creature you are making, you may also need other types of fabric and a selection of trimmings, including buttons. The exact requirements for each monster are given on the individual project pages.

FLEECE FABRIC
The monsters are made from standard fleece fabric. Fleece is available in a variety of thicknesses and finishes. Medium-weight fleece with a slight pile is ideal for making fleecie creatures as thin fabrics can be too stretchy and thick fabrics too difficult to work with.

give your own old clothes a second lease of life by transforming them into fleecie monsters!

POLYESTER FILLING

This 100 per cent polyester filling is manufactured specially for stuffing soft toys, cushions and other handmade items. It is widely available in craft and haberdashery shops. Always check that the filling you are buying is marked safe and washable and that it conforms to safety standards.

PATTERNED COTTONS

For some of the monsters you will need small amounts of printed fabrics in 100 per cent cotton or cotton mixes (a blend of polyester and cotton). You don't need to use exactly the same fabric shown in the project. But the fabric you use will determine the finished look and character of your monster, so spend a bit of time selecting a fabric that you really like and that you think will work well.

FELT

Felt is used for some of the monsters' features. There are two main types of craft felt, both of them widely available and sold in squares measuring about 23 x 23 cm (9 x 9 in) in craft, haberdashery and fabric shops. The first type is made from 100 per cent polyester and the second type from a mixture of viscose and wool. I would recommend that you try to find the felt made from viscose and wool because it is slightly thinner and easier to cut into small shapes. Some craft shops also sell ready-cut felt circles and shapes which

Good quality fleece fabric usually has a pile, which makes it smoother when it is stroked in one direction than any other. It is important when making the cutting and sewing that the direction of the pile runs down the length of the creature.

Fleece fabric in a good range of colours is available in many dress fabric shops, and there are some attractive patterned designs as well. But if there isn't a good fabric shop near you, don't worry. There are plenty of mail order and internet companies offering this type of fabric at competitive prices, and it is often available through individual sellers and stores on Ebay.

If you want an even greater choice of colours and textures – and want to save money at the same time – you could look at fleece clothing in budget and second-hand shops. You could even you may find useful for the creatures' eyes in some of the projects.

EMBROIDERY THREAD
Some of the monsters' features are embroidered with 100 per cent cotton stranded embroidery thread. The strands can be easily separated. Most of the projects use either six or three strands.

SEWING THREAD
Whether you are sewing with a machine or by hand, you will need standard sewing threads to match your fabrics. Threads made from 100 per cent polyester, often called 'all purpose' are widely available and come in a good range of colours. While it is not essential to go for the very best quality threads, it is important to avoid very poor quality, cheap threads as they can break easily and are prone to puckering.

BONDING WEB
For some of the creatures you will need a small amount of fusible bonding web to fasten the appliqués. Bonding web is a thin web of dry glue that is fixed on a paper backing. The shape for the appliqué is traced onto the paper backing (smooth side) with a standard pencil. The bonding web is then ironed onto the reverse side of the fabric and cut out. The backing can then be peeled off and the appliqué pressed in place with an iron. There are several brands of bonding web on sale and it is widely available in craft and haberdashery shops.

SEAM SEALANT
Seam sealant is a special type of clear liquid that is sold in a small bottle with a pointed nozzle that has a narrow opening. It is used in some of the projects to prevent trimmings from fraying. Although the sealant is fine to use on most trimmings, it's a good idea to test it on a scrap of the trimming first. Seam sealant is widely available in craft and haberdashery shops.

TRIMMINGS AND BUTTONS
For some of the projects you will need buttons, ribbons and other trimmings. You should be able to find a good selection of these in your local craft or haberdashery shop or at internet companies that specialise in fabrics and trimmings or greetings card making. Second-hand stores are also a great source of these items – especially buttons. The trimmings you select are crucial to your project and choosing the right ones will help make sure that your fleecie monsters look great. So take your time when deciding which ones to use. You will find it really helpful if you build up your own collection as this will enable you to try out various styles before deciding which is your favourite.

SAFETY

It is very important that you do not give any of the monsters with added extras, such as buttons, to children under three years old as these can be a choking hazard. All of the creatures can be easily adapted to suit younger children. For example, you can use eyes made from coloured circles of felt instead of buttons.

Techniques

PREPARING YOUR TEMPLATES

All the templates you need for making the monsters in this book are provided and shown actual size. The easiest way to prepare your template is to use a photocopier or to scan it into a computer using a flat bed scanner. Simply photocopy the templates you need onto thick paper or thin card (card stock) or scan them into your computer and print them out onto thick paper or thin card. In some cases the templates have been split over two pages; simply join at the dotted lines and tape together.

TRANSFERRING YOUR TEMPLATE TO YOUR FABRIC

You can transfer your template to your fabric by holding the template firmly in position on the reverse side of your fabric and drawing around it using a water-soluble pen or quilter's pencil. You can use the same pen or pencil to mark the positions of the dots, which act as guidelines for sewing and making your monsters. Simply poke the pen nib or pencil tip through the template or make a hole in the template first using a large needle.

BASIC SEWING SKILLS

If you are sewing your monsters by machine, you will need to use a medium length straight stitch to sew your monsters together and to stitch their clothes. The instructions for some of the monsters also recommend that you use zig zag stitch if your machine has this option, though this is not essential. If you are using zig zag stitch, it is a good idea to test it out first on a scrap of material so you can check that you are pleased with the size and spacing of the stitching.

If you are sewing by hand, use a standard 'sharps' sewing needle and a small running stitch. Work a small back stitch every few stitches for extra strength.

To secure your work at the beginning and end, work a few stitches on top of each other if you are sewing by hand. If you are using a sewing machine, most machines have a reverse direction so you can sew a short length of reverse stitching before you begin and after you complete your sewing to secure the stitches in place.

Basting (Tacking)

Because fleece and felt are not slippery fabrics, most of the monsters can be completed by simply pinning the pieces of work together before sewing. For some steps in some of the projects, however, it is easier if you baste your fabric first. Basting stitches are temporary stitches that are pulled out after your work is finished. They are large running stitches and, so long as they are holding your work in position securely, they don't have to be particularly even or tidy. It is sensible to baste in a contrasting colour thread so that you can easily tell which threads to pull out.

Sewing Your Monster Using Corresponding Pieces

This book uses a slightly different technique for sewing pieces together than many other books. For example, instead of cutting two pieces of a main body shape, you are asked to cut just one piece and then to cut a corresponding shape – a second piece of fabric that roughly matches the original piece. You place your original piece face down on the corresponding piece before sew the pieces together. Then you trim your fabric to match your shape before turning your work the right way out.

Sewing your toys in this way is both quicker and easier. And even if you aren't experienced at sewing, you can achieve great results because you won't find holes in your seams or uneven work, even if your fabric has slipped or stretched slightly.

Stuffing

Always use a small amount of toy filling at a time when you are stuffing your monsters. Also, try not to push each bit in too hard or your creature will look lumpy. The monsters should look fully stuffed but have a nice squashy feel. You can push the stuffing into the creatures using the blunt end of a pencil or something similar – but make sure that you don't use anything too sharp or push too hard or you might break the stitching.

Slip Stitch and Closing Openings

Once your
monster has
been turned the
right way out and
stuffed, you will
need to close
the opening that
you have used
for stuffing. The
neatest way is to
slip stitch the two
edges together.

Fold in the raw edges on both sides
of the opening, in line with the seam line. From
the inside, bring your needle out through one side
of the fold at the beginning of the opening. Take
the needle in through the fold directly opposite
and out through the same fold, about 3 mm
(⅛ in) further along. Work a few stitches at a time
before pulling your thread taut. You will also need
to work similar slip stitches to turn up some of
the creatures' feet.

Oversewing

This stitch is used
to fasten some of
the felt and fleece
features such as
the monsters'
eyes, and to
sew on some of
the appliqués if
you are sewing

by hand. It is also used for joining some of the
creatures' limbs to their main bodies. Use small
stitches along the fabric edge or across two
pieces of fabric to join them together. Once the
thread is pulled fairly tightly, the stitches should
be virtually invisible on fleece. In the case of felt
features, use the point of a fine needle to tease
the fabric around the stitches to make them
barely noticeable.

SPECIAL EMBROIDERY STITCHES

For some of the monsters you will need to use special embroidery stitches. Instructions for these stitches are given below.

BACK STITCH

This is used to work some of the monsters' mouths. To work a row of back stitch, bring your thread out at your starting point and start by working a single running stitch. Insert your

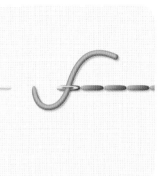

needle back into the end point of the first stitch then out again, a little further on from the end of the last stitch.

CHAIN STITCH

This is used to work some of the monsters' mouths and some of their teeth. First, bring your needle out at the point where you want the chain to start. Insert the needle back into the

same hole and out at the point you want the stitch

to end – about 2 or 3 mm (⅛ in) further on – making sure the thread is under the needle point.

Now pull the thread through. You are now ready to start the second stitch.

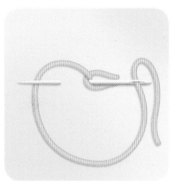

At the end of the row, make a small stitch over the last loop to hold it in position. If you are just working single chain stitches, simply make the small loop over the single stitch to hold it in position.

Blanket Stitch

You will use this stitch around the edge of some of the appliquéd pieces on the creatures if you are sewing by hand, as an alternative to machine zig zag stitching.

To begin, take your needle out at your starting point. Then insert your needle back through your fabric, a stitch width to the side. Now bring the needle round the back of the edge, directly above this point.

Work around the edge of the piece in the same way, taking care to make your stitches the same height and width.

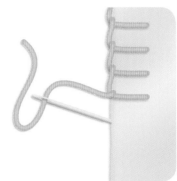

Make sure your thread is under the needle point and pull up gently to make the first stitch.

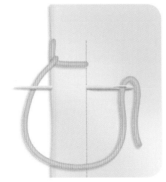

A NOTE ON MEASUREMENT

All the measurements are given in metric units (millimetres or centimetres) with the imperial measurement in inches and fractions of an inch given afterwards. It is difficult to convert small measurements exactly so figures have been rounded up or down, usually to the nearest 5 mm (¼ in). Because it is impossible to make the conversions exact, it is important that you follow one system only rather than mix the two.

Rory the Rabbit

Materials
- one glove
- sewing thread
- buttons
- one sock
- polyester toy stuffing

Tools
- scissors
- sewing needle

If you have an odd glove and an old sock lying around, transform them into a cuddly companion.

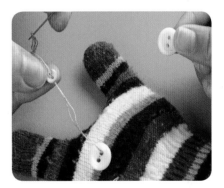

2 Sew up the gaps and turn right sides out. Sew on buttons for eyes.

1 Turn the glove inside out and cut off the thumb and middle two fingers.

SAFETY
When making this toy for a very small child, you may prefer not to use buttons as these can come off and become a swallowing hazard.

3 Cut a 15 cm (6 in) length from the leg of the sock. Turn inside out. Make two 4 cm (2½ in) snips at one end, on opposite sides.

4 Put a little bit of stuffing into the two fingers than were removed from the glove and place the cut edges in the slits, with the finger inside the sock. Stitch in place.

5 Turn right sides out and sew on buttons. Sew a gathering thread around the top of the 'body', draw up to gather slightly, slip neck (cuff of glove) inside and stitch together.

6 Stuff the head and body and stitch up the opening at the base.

COOL IDEA
The finished result will vary according to the sizes, shapes and colours of the glove and sock you have available, allowing plenty of scope for creativity.

Leo

Leo is approximately 22 cm (8¾ in) tall.

Playful Leo does his best to snarl and adopt a menacing stance and he'd like people to think he is really scary. But, as everyone knows, he's just a big softie – and actually, he's not even all that big!

MATERIALS
• a piece of bright red fleece, 34 x 45 cm (13½ x 17¾ in). If the fabric has an obvious pile this should run down its longer length.
• a scrap of beige fleece for the face
• a scrap of pale pink felt for the mouth
• two medium odd buttons for the eyes
• lime green embroidery thread for the claws
• 20 g (¾ oz) polyester toy stuffing
• matching threads for your fabrics including the felt
• black sewing thread for machine stitching the mouth (or black embroidery thread if you want to sew the features by hand)

TOOLS
• access to a photocopier or computer with scanner and printer
• scissors
• sewing needles
• dressmaking pins
• water-soluble pen or quilter's pencil
• sewing machine (optional)

1 Photocopy or scan the templates provided for making Leo and cut them out. Place the red fleece right side down on a flat surface. Position your templates on top and draw around them with the water-soluble pen or quilter's pencil. You will need to cut out one body, two legs and two arms. Make sure that any pile on

2 Place the face on the body shape in the position indicated on the template, making sure that any obvious pile goes downwards, and pin or baste in position. Sew around the face using a medium zig zag stitch if your machine has this option. Alternatively, use an ordinary machine stitch or oversew in place by hand. If you are sewing by machine, it's a good idea to start your stitching in the middle of one side of the face where the join will be least noticeable.

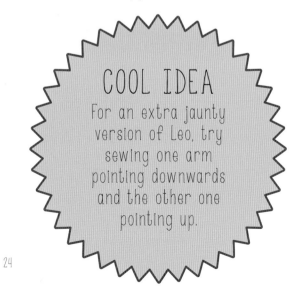

COOL IDEA

For an extra jaunty version of Leo, try sewing one arm pointing downwards and the other one pointing up.

3 Use the template to cut out the mouth from pale pink felt and position as indicated on the template. Pin or baste in place and sew around the mouth in matching thread using a small zig zag stitch if your machine has this option. Alternatively use a machine running stitch or oversew it in place using tiny stitches. Work the mouth in a large machine zig zag stitch, going over your work two or three times to make the mouth stand out. Alternatively, embroider a row of zig zag stitches using three strands of black embroidery thread. If you are embroidering the mouth by hand, you may find it useful to draw a guideline first using the water-soluble pen or quilter's pencil.

4 Place one of the arm pieces onto its corresponding piece of fleece, making sure that the right sides are together and any obvious pile on the corresponding fabric is going in the same direction as the main piece. Sew around the arm shape 5 mm (¼ in) from the edge, leaving the flat end open for turning and stuffing. Trim away the excess fabric on the corresponding piece of fleece so that it matches the original arm. Trim the fleece particularly close to the seams around the fingers and make small clips between the fingers, taking care not to cut into the seam (this will help give the finished fingers a smooth shape). Complete the second arm and both legs in the same way. Turn the arms and legs the right way out and stuff.

5 Now place the body piece face down on its corresponding piece of fleece, making sure that the pieces are right sides together and any obvious pile on the corresponding fabric is going in the same direction as the main piece. Sew around the body 5 mm (¼ in) from the edge, leaving openings between the dots for inserting the arms and legs and for turning and stuffing. Trim away the excess fabric.

6 Turn the body the right way out and stuff. Close the opening used for turning and stuffing using slip stitch.

7 Insert about 5 mm (¼ in) of the top of one of the arms into the opening at the side of the body. Secure by oversewing across the front and back of the arm top. Position and secure the other arm and both legs in the same way. Using the photograph of the finished monster as a guide, sew on the two button eyes.

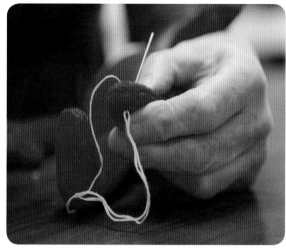

8 To make the feet, turn up 5 cm (2 in) at the end of each leg and hold in place so that the foot is at a right angle to the leg. Now, using the thread double for strength and starting at one of the side seams, work a few large, loose slip stitches across the curve at the front of the ankle. Pull up the thread fairly tightly and secure.

9 For the claws, use three strands of lime green embroidery thread. Secure the thread invisibly in the side seam and take the needle out through the top of the foot ready to sew the first claw. Now take the thread over the end of the foot, through the back and out through the top again, ready to work the next claw. Work two more claws the same way and secure the thread in the side seam.

Quincy

Quincy is approximately 15 cm (6 in) tall.

Quincy is one unique fleecie creature! He has all the fluffy appeal of a favourite teddy bear – but there's a definite hint of octopus in him as well. Although he looks as if he'd be hard to put together, Quincy is made from just two main pattern pieces – so please give him a go.

Materials

- a piece of orange fleece, 35 x 35 cm
- a scrap of lime fleece for the face
- scraps of black and white felt for the eyes
- 20 g (¾ oz) polyester toy stuffing
- matching threads for your fabrics including the felt, plus red thread for the mouth
- seam sealant for preventing ric rac from fraying (optional)

Tools

- access to a photocopier or computer with scanner and printer
- scissors
- sewing needles
- dressmaking pins
- water-soluble pen or quilter's pencil
- sewing machine (optional)

1 Photocopy or scan the templates provided and cut them out. Place the orange fleece right side down on a flat surface. Position your templates on top and draw around them with the water-soluble pen or quilter's pencil. You will need to cut out one head and one leg, remembering to mark the position of the dots. For the head, make sure that any pile on the fabric runs down the length of the piece in the direction of the arrows shown on the template. You will also need to cut shapes that roughly match these pieces (for more information, see introduction), bearing in mind the direction of the pile. From the lime fleece, cut out one face panel.

2 Place the face panel on the head following the template as a guide, and making sure that any obvious pile goes downwards, and pin or baste in position. Sew around the face using a small zig zag stitch if your machine has this option. Alternatively, use an ordinary machine stitch or oversew by hand. If you are sewing by machine, it's a good idea to start your stitching in the middle of one side of the face so any join will be hidden by the felt eye.

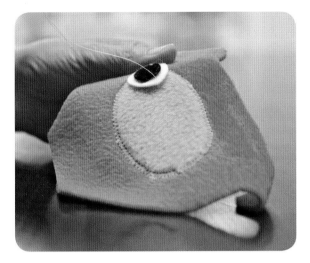 

3 Treat the ends of the ric rac braid with seam sealant and leave to dry completely. Meanwhile, use the templates to cut out two outer eyes in white felt and two inner eyes in black felt. Using the template as a guide, oversew the eyes in place using tiny stitches. When you have finished, gently tease around the stitches with the tip of your needle so that they become almost invisible.

4 Using the photograph as a guide, now pin or baste the ric rac braid mouth in position. Machine stitch along the middle of the ric rac braid using red thread. Work two rows, one on top of the other, to make sure the stitching stands out. If sewing by hand, back stitch along the braid using your thread double.

 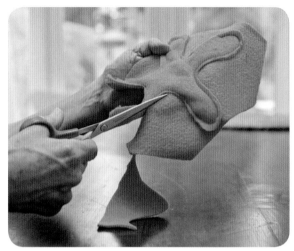

5 Place the head face down on the corresponding piece of fabric making sure that the two pieces of fabric are right sides together and that any obvious pile on the corresponding fabric is going in the same direction as the main piece. Stitch around the shape, 5 mm (¼ in) from the edge, leaving it open at the lower edge for turning and stuffing. Trim away the excess fabric. Turn the head right side out and stuff.

6 Place the leg on the corresponding piece of fabric making sure that the two pieces of fabric are right sides together. Stitch around the shape, 5 mm (¼ in) from the edge, leaving an opening between the dots for turning and stuffing. Trim away the excess fabric. Turn the leg piece the right side out and stuff. Close the opening used for turning and stuffing using slip stitch.

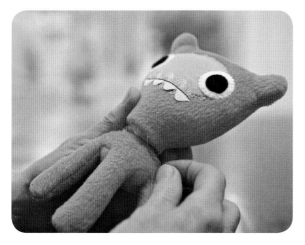

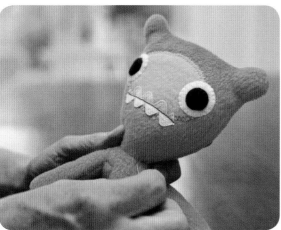

COOL IDEA
To give Quincy a skittish look, try sewing some of his legs folded down and some folded upwards.

7 Place the head onto the centre of the legs and slip stitch in position, slightly opening out the neck edge as you go so that the base of the neck forms a circle shape on the top of the legs.

8 Working from the underneath, fold each leg up slightly. Using your thread double for strength, sew a few large slip stitches across the fold of each leg to secure in position.

Martha

Martha is approximately 25 cm (10 in) tall.

Cuddly Martha with her flowery tummy patch loves the countryside. She probably likes nothing better than hopping about the fields and wildflowers on her big feet. But something tells me she'd feel just as much at home on a nice flowery pink quilt or soft cushion.

MATERIALS

• a piece of bright pink fleece, 28 x 40 cm (11 x 16 in). If the fabric has an obvious pile this should run down its longer length.
• a piece of pale pink fleece, 21 x 17 cm (8¼ x 6¾ in). If the fabric has an obvious pile this should run down its longer length.
• scraps of black and white felt for the eyes
• a small piece of medium-weight cotton or cotton/linen mix floral print fabric for the tummy patch and ears
• a small piece of bonding web
• a small black button for the nose
• dark grey embroidery thread
• 35 g (1¼ oz) polyester toy stuffing
• matching threads for your fabrics and felt

TOOLS

• access to a photocopier or computer with scanner and printer
• scissors
• ordinary pencil
• sewing needles
• dressmaking pins
• water-soluble pen or quilter's pencil
• sewing machine (optional)
• iron
• a piece of fine cotton such as a handkerchief to protect the appliqué when fixing with the iron

1 Photocopy or scan the templates provided for making Martha and cut them out (you don't need to cut out the tummy patch template). Place the bright pink fleece right side down on a flat surface. Position your templates on top and draw around them with the water-soluble pen or quilter's pencil. You will need to cut out two body pieces, two legs and two arms. Make sure that any pile on the fabric runs down the length of the fabric in the direction of the arrow shown on the templates and remember to mark the position of the dots. You will also need to cut shapes that roughly match the arms and legs (see introduction), bearing in mind the direction of the pile. From the pale pink fleece, cut out two heads. Cut out four ears from floral fabric.

2 To make the tummy appliqué, trace around the tummy patch template onto the backing paper of a piece of bonding web using a pencil. Next, with the iron on a warm setting, iron the bonding web onto the reverse of your piece of fabric and cut the shape out carefully. Peel off the backing paper and position the patch on the body, as shown on the template. Place a piece of fine cotton over the template and iron to fix. You might find it easier to iron on the reverse of the body piece to do this. Sew around the appliqué using a small zig zag stitch if your machine has this option. Alternatively, use an ordinary machine running stitch. If sewing by hand, use a small blanket stitch worked with your thread double.

3 Use the templates provided to draw and cut out two outer eyes from white felt and two inner eyes from black felt with the small embroidery scissors. Using the template as a guide, oversew the eyes in place using tiny stitches. Using the template as a guide again, embroider the mouth in chain stitch using three strands of dark grey embroidery thread. You will find it easier to sew if you draw an outline using your water-soluble pen or quilter's pencil before you begin. Make a row of five separate, large running stitches for the eyelashes, again using three strands of dark grey embroidery thread. Sew on the button nose.

4 Place one of the arm pieces onto its corresponding piece of fleece, making sure that the right sides are together and any obvious pile on the corresponding fabric is going in the same direction as the main piece. Sew around the arm shape 5 mm (¼ in) from the edge, leaving the flat end open for turning. Trim away the excess fabric on the corresponding piece of fleece so that it matches the original arm shape. Complete the second arm and both legs in the same way. Turn the arms and legs the right way out and stuff the legs but not the arms.

5 Place two of the ear pieces right sides together and sew around the curved edge leaving a 5 mm (¼ in) seam allowance. Clip into the seam allowance, taking care not to cut the stitching (this will help give the finished ear a smooth shape). Turn the ear the right way out and press. Complete the second ear in the same way.

6 Sew the head piece with the facial features to the body piece with the tummy patch, catching in the arms where indicated on the template, and leaving a 5 mm (¼ in) seam allowance. Sew the back head and body pieces together in the same way, leaving a gap between the dots for stuffing.

7 For the ears, fold the two lower corners towards the middle so that, for the left-hand ear, the left corner overlaps the right and, for the right-hand ear, the right corner overlaps the left.

8 Baste the ears onto the head piece in the position indicated on the template, lining up the flat raw edge of the ears with the raw edge at the top of the head so that the ears point down the head. Place the two body pieces right sides together, checking that the side seams line up, and stitch around the complete creature in matching threads 5 mm (¼ in) from the edge, leaving openings between the dots for inserting the legs. Turn right side out through the gap at the back. Stuff your creature then slip stitch the opening closed.

9 Insert about 5 mm (¼ in) of the top of one of the legs into the opening at the bottom of the body. Secure by oversewing across the front and back of the leg top. Position and secure the other leg in the same way.

10 To make the feet, turn up 6 cm (2½ in) at the end of each leg and hold in place so that the foot is at a right angle to the leg. Now, using the thread double for strength and starting at one of the side seams, work a few large, loose slip stitches across the curve at the front of the ankle. Pull up the thread fairly tightly and secure.

11 For the claws, use three strands of dark grey embroidery thread. Secure the thread invisibly in the side seam and take the needle out through the top of the foot ready to sew the first claw. Now take the thread over the end of the foot, through the back and out through the top again, ready to work the next claw. Work two more claws the same way and secure the thread in the side seam.

COOL IDEA

For a cat-like version of Martha, try sewing two simple triangular ears instead of the bunny-like ears shown here.

Dinah and Daughter

Dinah is approximately 29 cm (11½ in) tall and her daughter is approximately 21 cm (8¼ in) tall.

MATERIALS

• a piece of bright green fleece, 30 x 40 cm (12 x 16 in). If the fabric has an obvious pile this should run down its shorter length.
• a piece of mid-pink fleece, 17 x 6 cm (6¾ x 2½ in)
• a scrap of yellow felt for the eye
• a 15 mm (¾ in) button for the eye
• 30 g (1 oz) polyester toy stuffing
• matching threads for your fabrics except the yellow felt

TOOLS

• access to a photocopier or computer with scanner and printer
• scissors
• sewing needles
• dressmaking pins
• water-soluble pen or quilter's pencil
• sewing machine (optional)

Dinah's ancestors were clearly dinosaurs. But with her soft pink spikes and colourful eye, Dinah is a whole lot less scary than her prehistoric forebears. However she still likes to scream and shout a bit.

COOL IDEA

Dinah is one of the easiest projects to make. To make her daughter, simply reduce the pattern by about a quarter - though make the flower eye the same size. Sew in exactly the same way as for Dinah but try to keep your seam allowance to approximately 3 mm (1/8 in).

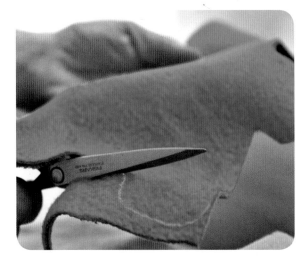 

1 Copy and cut out the templates provided for Dinah. Place the green fleece right side down on a flat surface. Centre the template on top and draw around it with the water-soluble pen or quilter's pencil. Cut out one body shape. Make sure that any pile on the fabric runs down the length of the piece in the direction of the arrow shown on the template and remember to mark the position of the dots. Cut a shape that roughly matches the body piece (for more information, see techniques), bearing in mind the direction of the pile.

2 Draw around the spikes template on the wrong side of the pink fleece using the water-soluble pen or quilter's pencil but do not cut out just yet. Sew just inside the cutting line of the spikes using a small zig zag stitch using a sewing machine. Alternatively, use a straight machine or hand running stitch. Trim very close to the stitching using embroidery scissors, taking care not to cut the stitching itself.

4 Now place the body piece on the corresponding piece of fleece, making sure that the pieces are right sides together and any obvious pile on the corresponding fabric is going in the same direction as the main piece. Sew around the body piece 5 mm (¼ in) from the edge, leaving an opening between the dots for turning and stuffing. Trim away the excess fabric. Turn the body the right way out and stuff. Close the opening used for turning and stuffing using slip stitch (see techniques).

3 Arrange the spikes on the right side of the body shape, between the dots on the template, so that the spikes face inwards and the flat edge lines up with the flat edge of the body. If your fleece has an obvious front and back and you want a monster facing right (like Dinah), place the spikes right sides up when you pin them to the body. For a monster facing left (like Dinah's daughter), arrange the spikes right side down. Baste the spikes in position.

5 For Dinah's eye, use the template to cut out a flower from the yellow felt using small embroidery scissors. Using the template as a guide, position the flower eye in place and secure using the button.

Zoltan

Zoltan is approximately 20 cm (8 in) long.

A little bit dragon, a touch of chameleon and a good dash of lizard – Zoltan certainly has exotic ancestry. You'll have to try to keep on the right side of him as he can get huffy quite easily. But if you're nice to him, he's a good creature to have on your side.

MATERIALS

• a piece of purple fleece, 25 x 42 cm (10 x 16½ in). If the fabric has an obvious pile this should run down its longer length.
• a piece of orange fleece, 5 x 20 cm (2 x 8 in) for the spikes
• a small piece of lime green fleece for the body markings
• scraps of black and white felt for the eye
• bright pink embroidery thread for the mouth
• 20 g (¾ oz) polyester toy stuffing
• matching threads for your fabrics including the felt

TOOLS

• access to a photocopier or computer with scanner and printer
• scissors
• sewing needles
• dressmaking pins
• water-soluble pen or quilter's pencil
• sewing machine (optional)

1 Photocopy or scan the templates provided for making Zoltan and cut them out. Place the purple fleece right side down on a flat surface. Position your template on top and draw around it with the water-soluble pen or quilter's pencil. If you want Zoltan to face right, as in the photograph, use the template face down. If you want your creature to face left, use the template the right way up. You will need to cut out just one body shape at this stage. Make sure that any pile on the fabric runs down the length of the piece in the direction of the arrow shown on the template and remember to mark the position of the dots. You will also need to cut a shape that roughly matches the body piece (for more information, see techniques), bearing in mind the direction of the pile. Cut out the body markings shape from lime green fleece, making sure any pile runs down the length of the piece, as shown on the template.

2 Position the body markings onto the body, as indicated on the template and stitch in place. Use a small zig zag stitch if your machine has this option. Alternatively, use an ordinary machine stitch or oversew by hand.

3 Draw around the spikes template on the reverse side of the orange fleece using the water-soluble pen or quilter's pencil but do not cut out just yet. Sew just inside the cutting line of the spikes using a small zig zag stitch on a sewing machine. Alternatively, use a straight machine or hand running stitch. Trim very close to the stitching using embroidery scissors, taking care not to cut the stitching itself.

4 Arrange the spikes right side down on the right side of the body shape, along the line indicated on the template at the top of the body, so that the spikes face inwards and the long, lower flat edge of the spikes lines up with the flat edge of the body. The longer spikes should be at the head end of the body. Baste the spikes in position.

5 Cut one outer eye from white felt and one inner eye from black felt. Using the template as a guide, oversew the eye pieces in place using tiny stitches. When you have finished, gently tease around the stitches with the tip of a needle so that your stitches become almost invisible.

6 Now place the body piece face down on the corresponding piece of fleece, making sure that the pieces are right sides together and any obvious pile on the corresponding fabric is going in the same direction as the main piece. Sew around the body piece 5 mm (¼ in) from the edge, leaving an opening between the dots for turning and stuffing. Trim away the excess fabric. Turn the body the right way out and stuff. Close the opening used for turning and stuffing using slip stitch.

7 For Zoltan's mouth, work a row of small chain stitches using three strands of bright pink embroidery thread.

COOL IDEA
If you don't fancy sewing Zoltan's spikes and want to save a bit of time, try sewing small loops of ribbon along his back instead.

Albert

Albert is approximately 26 cm (10¼ in) tall.

With the quirky appeal of a strange species of duck, Albert is the perfect fleecie monster for bird lovers everywhere. With his smart striped breast and curvy yellow wings, he stands tall and proud. Best of all, he will never utter a single annoying quack.

MATERIALS

- a piece of orange fleece, 16 x 28 cm (6¼ x 11 in). If the fabric has an obvious pile this should run down its shorter length.
- a piece of yellow fleece, 28 x 14 cm (11 x 5½ in). If the fabric has an obvious pile this should run down its shorter length.
- a small piece of red fleece
- a small piece of multicolour striped fleece for the breast
- a scrap of lime green fleece or felt for the eye
- two odd buttons for the eyes – one about 17 mm (¾ in) diameter and the other about 11 mm (½ in) diameter
- 30 g (1 oz) polyester toy stuffing
- matching threads for your fabrics (except for the lime fleece or felt for the eye)

TOOLS

- access to a photocopier or computer with scanner and printer
- scissors
- sewing needles
- dressmaking pins
- water-soluble pen or quilter's pencil
- sewing machine (optional)

1 Photocopy or scan the templates provided for making Albert and cut them out. Place the orange fleece right side down on a flat surface. Position the body template on top and draw around it with the water-soluble pen or quilter's pencil. You will need to cut out two body shapes from the orange fleece. Make sure that any pile on the fabric runs down the length of the pieces in the direction of the arrows shown on the templates and remember to mark the position of the dots. From the red fleece, cut out two face pieces – one using the template the right way up and one using it face down. From the striped fleece, cut out one tummy patch. From the yellow fleece, cut out two legs, two wings and two beaks. You will also need to cut shapes that roughly match the legs and wings (for more information, see techniques), bearing in mind the direction of the pile.

2 Place the two wings face up on the wrong side of the corresponding pieces of yellow fleece, making sure that any pile is going in the same direction on all pieces. Using a machine or hand running stitch, sew around the wings about 5 mm (¼ in) from the edge, leaving the flat edge open. Trim away the excess fabric on the corresponding pieces of fleece so that each matches the original wing shapes.

COOL IDEA
To make Albert really funky, try designing your own cockerel comb.

3 Place one of the legs onto its corresponding piece of fleece, making sure that the right sides are together and any obvious pile on the corresponding fabric is going in the same direction as the main piece. Sew around the leg 5 mm (¼ in) from the edge, leaving the top end open for turning and stuffing. Trim away the excess fabric on the corresponding piece of fleece so that it matches the original leg shape. Complete the second leg in the same way. Turn the legs the right way out and stuff.

4 Place the tummy patch in the centre of one of the body pieces, making sure that any obvious pile goes downwards, and pin or baste in position. Sew around the patch using a small zig zag stitch if your machine has this option. Alternatively, use an ordinary machine stitch or oversew by hand. Place the beak pieces right side down on the face pieces so that the flat edges line up and the beak points towards the back of the head. Sew together leaving a 5 mm (¼ in) seam allowance. If you want Albert to face right, as shown in the photo, position the green outer eye on the head piece with the beak pointing right, using the position guide shown on the template. If you want Albert facing left, sew his eye to the head piece with the beak pointing left. Sew in place using a machine or hand running stitch and red thread.

5 Seam the two head pieces to the two body pieces in matching threads, remembering to sew the head shape with the eye piece to the body shape with the tummy patch and leaving a 5 mm (¼ in) seam allowance. Remember to leave an opening between the dots for turning and stuffing the pieces that will form the reverse of the creature, as indicated on the template.

6 Position the wings along the sides of the creature, as shown on the template, so that the curved sections point inwards and the raw edges of the wings line up with the raw edges of the body. Baste in position. Place the two creature shapes right sides together, checking that the neck and beak seams line up, and stitch around the complete creature in matching threads, 5 mm (¼ in) from the edge, leaving openings between the dots for inserting the legs. Turn the right way out through the gap at the back of the neck. Stuff, then slip stitch the opening closed.

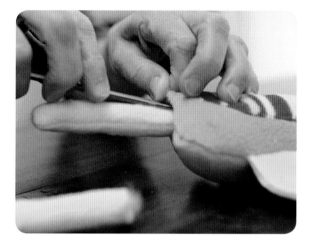

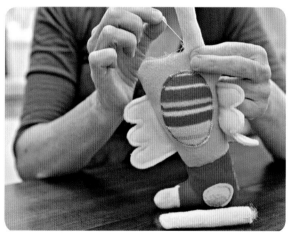

8 To make the feet, turn up 4 cm (1½ in) at the end of each leg and hold in place so that the foot is at a right angle to the leg. Now, using your thread double for strength and starting at one of the side seams, work a few large, loose slip stitches across the curve at the front of the ankle. Pull up the thread fairly tightly and secure.

9 Complete Albert by sewing the two buttons in place, one on top of the other, as shown in the photograph.

7 Insert about 5 mm (¼ in) of the top of one of the legs into the opening at the bottom of the body. Secure by oversewing across the front and back of the leg top. Position and secure the other leg in the same way.

Three Mini Monsters

Wilf, Prudence and Melvin are each approximately 13 cm (5¼ in) tall.

Wilf, Prudence and Melvin are three cute little guys that you can fit in your pocket. Now, you'll never need to be without a fleecie monster, wherever you are!

MATERIALS

WILF
• a piece of lime green fleece, 28 x 16 cm (11 x 6¼ in). If the fabric has an obvious pile this should run down its shorter length.
• a scrap of dark grey felt for the eyes
• a scrap of pale pink felt for the mouth
• white embroidery thread for the teeth
• bright pink embroidery thread for the eye
• 15 g (½ oz) polyester toy stuffing
• matching threads for your fabrics

PRUDENCE
• a piece of bright pink fleece, 34 x 16 cm (13½ x 6¼ in). If the fabric has an obvious pile this should run down its shorter length.
• a scrap of yellow fleece for the face panel
• a scrap of black felt for the eyes
• orange embroidery thread for the mouth
• 15 g (½ oz) polyester toy stuffing
• matching threads for your fabrics

MELVIN
• a piece of orange fleece, 28 x 16 cm (11 x 6¼ in). If the fabric has an obvious pile this should run down the shorter length of the fabric.
• an odd cream button for one of the eyes
• turquoise embroidery thread for the other eye
• dark grey embroidery thread for the mouth
• a scrap of white felt for the teeth
15 g (½ oz) polyester toy stuffing
• matching threads for your fabrics

TOOLS

• access to a photocopier or computer with scanner and printer
• scissors
• sewing needles
• dressmaking pins
• water-soluble pen or quilter's pencil
• sewing machine (optional)

Wilf

1 Photocopy or scan the templates provided for making Wilf and cut them out. Place the lime green fleece right side down on a flat surface. Position your template on top and draw around it with the water-soluble pen or quilter's pencil. You will need to cut out one body shape only at this stage. Make sure that any pile on the fabric runs down the length of the piece in the direction of the arrow shown on the template and remember to mark the position of the dots. You will also need to cut a shape that roughly matches the body piece, bearing in mind the direction of the pile. Cut out the mouth from pale pink felt and the eyes from the dark grey felt.

2 Position the mouth, as shown on the template and oversew in place using tiny stitches. Place and sew the eyes in the same way. Gently tease around the stitches with the tip of your needle so that the stitches become almost invisible.

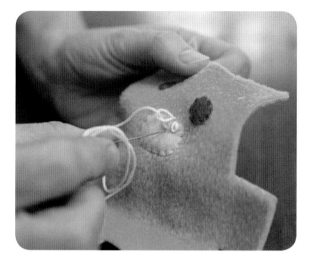

3 Embroider the teeth with six strands of white stranded cotton, using single chain stitch. With six strands of bright pink embroidery thread and large running stitches, work a star shape over the larger eye.

4 Place the body piece face down on its corresponding piece of fleece, making sure that the pieces are right sides together and any obvious pile on the corresponding fabric is going in the same direction as the main piece. Sew round the body piece 5 mm (¼ in) from the edge, leaving an opening between the dots for turning and stuffing. Trim away the excess fabric to match the body shape. Turn the body the right way out and stuff. Close the opening used for turning and stuffing using slip stitch.

Prudence

1 Photocopy or scan the templates provided for making Prudence and cut them out. Place the bright pink fleece right side down on a flat surface. Position your template and draw around it with the water-soluble pen or quilter's pencil. You will need to cut out one body shape only at this stage. Make sure that any pile on the fabric runs down the length of the piece in the direction of the arrow shown on the template and remember to mark the position of the dots. You will also need to cut a shape that roughly matches the body piece (for more information, see techniques), bearing in mind the direction of the pile. Cut out the face from yellow fleece and the eyes from the black felt.

2 Place the face panel on the head as shown on the template, making sure that any obvious pile goes downwards, and pin or baste in position. Sew around the face using a small zig zag stitch if your machine has this option. Alternatively, use an ordinary machine stitch or oversew by hand.

3 Embroider the mouth in back stitch using six strands of orange embroidery thread. Position the eyes and oversew in place using tiny stitches). Gently tease around the stitches with the tip of a needle so they become almost invisible.

4 Now place the body piece face down on the corresponding piece of fleece, making sure that the pieces are right sides together and any obvious pile on the corresponding fabric is going in the same direction as the main piece. Sew around the body piece 5 mm (¼ in) from the edge, leaving an opening between the dots for turning and stuffing. Trim away the excess fabric. Turn the body the right way out and stuff. Close the opening used for turning and stuffing using slip stitch.

5 Squeeze the base of the ears inwards and secure the pleat with a couple of stitches.

Melvin

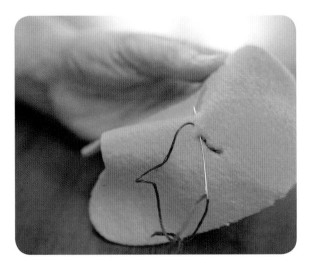

1 Photocopy or scan the template provided for making Melvin and cut it out. Place the orange fleece right side down on a flat surface. Position your template on top and draw around it with the water-soluble pen or quilter's pencil. You will need to cut out one body shape only at this stage. Make sure that any pile on the fabric runs down the length of the piece in the direction of the arrow shown on the template and remember to mark the position of the dots. You will also need to cut a shape that roughly matches the body piece (for more information, see techniques), bearing in mind the direction of the pile.

2 Using the template as a guide, embroider the mouth in chain stitch or back stitch using six strands of dark grey embroidery thread. You might find it helpful to draw the mouth shape with the water-soluble pen or quilter's pencil before you begin stitching.

COOL IDEA
Sew a short length of ribbon into the top seam when stitching the mini monsters together. Use your hanging mini monster to make a big funky key ring or a hanging decoration for a doorknob.

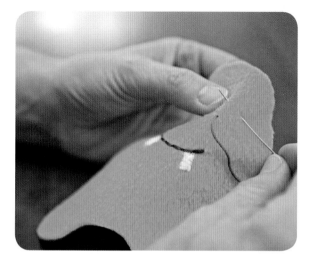 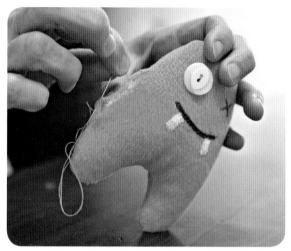

3 Cut two small rectangles of white felt for the teeth. Using the template as a guide, oversew in place using tiny stitches. Gently tease around the stitches with the tip of a needle. Work a single cross stitch for the right-hand eye using six strands of turquoise embroidery thread and sew on the button for the second eye.

4 Now place the body piece face down on its corresponding piece of fleece, making sure that the pieces are right sides together and any obvious pile is going in the same direction as the main piece. Sew around the body piece 5 mm (¼ in) from the edge, leaving an opening between the dots for turning and stuffing. Trim away the excess fabric to match the body shape. Turn the body the right way out and stuff. Close the opening used for turning and stuffing using slip stitch. Sew on the button for Melvin's second eye.

Penny Puppet

All you need to put on a puppet show are coloured felt scraps, a needle and some thread.

Materials
- coloured craft felt
- embroidery thread
- fabric glue

Tools
- scissors
- sewing needles

COOL IDEA
Little fingers need practice to get to grips with needle and thread. To speed up the process, some parts of the puppet can be attached using fabric glue.

1 For the body, place your finger on a double layer of felt and draw around it, making sure the shape is at least twice as wide as your finger. Alternatively, trace the templates provided on to paper and cut these out.

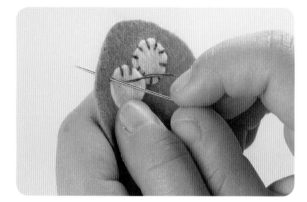

2 Cut out the felt pieces. Choose a piece for the front of the puppet and add circles for eyes. Stick or stitch these in place. Stitch eyes, mouth and other small details using embroidery thread.

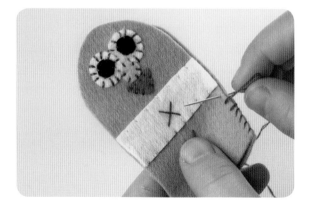

3 Now add other details such as clothes, cut from scraps of felt. Stitch the front and back of the finger puppet together. Do this by oversewing the sides or with a running stitch – whichever you find easier.

Sam the Sock Puppet

Materials

- long sock
- matching sewing thread
- 2 sew-on googly eyes
- few strands of fine cord
- small scraps of black and pink felt

Tools

- scissors
- sewing needle

Is it a dog, a cat or a leopard? It all depends on the colour and pattern of the sock you use, or on your imagination!

COOL IDEA

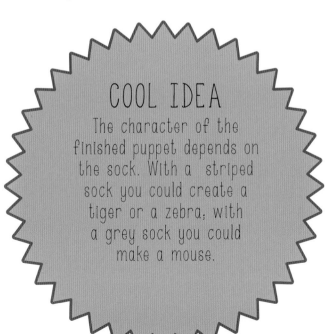

The character of the finished puppet depends on the sock. With a striped sock you could create a tiger or a zebra; with a grey sock you could make a mouse.

1 Turn the sock inside out. Flatten out the heel and cut out a V-shape from the centre, then stitch up cut edges to form ears. Turn right sides out.

2 Push in the toe end, to form a mouth. Thread the needle with a double strand of sewing thread and sew a running stitch all around the folded edge and pull up to gather. Fasten off.

3 Sew on eyes, then cut a few lengths of cord to form whiskers and stitch these in place in the top centre of the mouth.

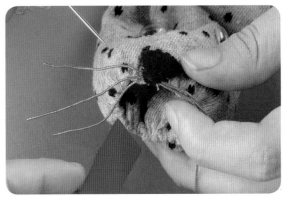

4 Cut a triangle of black felt and stitch on top of the place where the whiskers are attached, folding one point of the triangle over the folded edge of the mouth.

5 Cut a pink shape for a tongue and stitch in place inside the mouth.

Frosty

Materials

- white sock
- scrap of heavy interfacing
- polyester toy filling
- white sewing thread
- scraps of orange and black felt
- striped sock
- scraps of knitting yarn

Tools

- scissors
- sewing needle
- knitting needles

With a couple of odd socks and basic sewing skills, you can make your own little snowman.

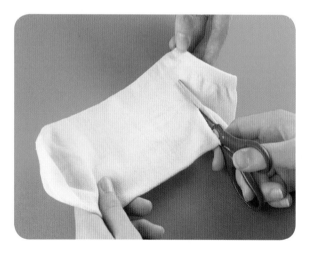

1 Cut across the top of the foot of the sock, just below the heel.

COOL IDEA
Why not use coloured socks to make other characters.

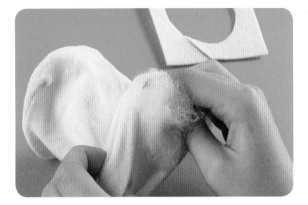

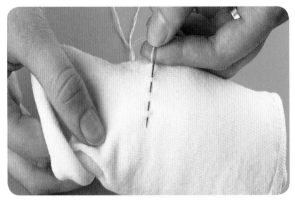

2 Cut a circle of interfacing, 6 cm (2½ in) in diameter, and push this into the toe of the sock, to form the base of the snowman. Stuff the body with polyester toy filling.

3 Thread the needle with two strands of white thread and attach the end of the thread to the sock, about 9 cm (3½ in) up from the base. Start to sew a running stitch.

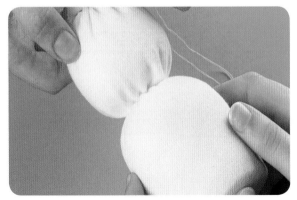

4 Sew the running stitch all around the sock and pull up to gather it; this forms the snowman's 'neck'.

5 Stuff the head then sew another line of running stitch about 5 mm (¼ in) from the top and pull up tightly. Fasten off.

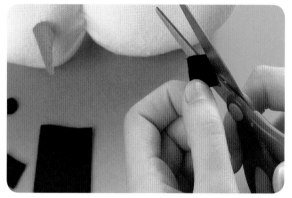

6 Cut a quarter-circle of orange felt. Roll it up into a cone and stitch to form a carrot nose.

7 Stitch the nose in place. Then cut small circles of black felt and stitch in place to form eyes, mouth and buttons.

8 To make a hat, cut off the top of a striped sock, 8 cm (3¾ in) from the top of the ribbing. Fold under the cut edge and sew a running thread all around, pulling up tightly to gather, then secure.

9 To make a scarf, cast on four stitches and knit until your work measures about 20 cm (8 in), then cast off.

Knitting

Introduction

This chapter features a fabulous collection of knitted and felted animals to make for a young person. Hand-knitted fabric lends itself so perfectly to toys; it's inherent softness and pliability is just waiting to be touched and cuddled. What could be nicer to welcome a new arrival or to indulge an adored child, than a lovable knitted companion?

There is something for everyone here, from bright and spotty Leo lion, to flowery Ellie the elephant. There's even a realistic and adorable little dog to make. Whatever project you choose, many are small enough to make good use of oddments of yarn leftover from other projects – just make sure that if you are going to felt your animal that there is a high percentage of pure wool in the yarn that you choose.

Some of the projects are suitable for those new to knitting – the mice, for instance. Once you're feeling confident, you can progress to more complex projects, just be sure to knit a tension square each time just to check that your project will turn out to the correct size. Happy knitting.

Tools and Materials

TOOLS

Before you start making these felted creatures you will need to check your knitting and general supplies for some basic equipment. As well as knitting needles you will find the following useful: a tape measure, safety pins, bobbins for colour knitting, scissors, pins and tapestry needles for sewing seams.

KNITTING NEEDLES

Knitting needles are available in a variety of materials from aluminium to wood, and come in sizes ranging from 2 mm to 10 mm and larger. They also come in a variety of lengths – what you use depends on personal preference. However, you may find it easier to use shorter needles for toy projects.

GLOSSARY OF UK AND US TERMINOLOGY

The following are the few differences between UK and US knitting terms:

UK	US
cast off	bind off
colour	shade
tension	gauge
moss stitch	seed stitch
stocking stitch	stockinette stitch
make up	finish
yarn over needle	yarn over (yo)
yarn forward	yarn over (yo)
yarn round needle	yarn over (yo)

YARN WEIGHT CONVERSION TABLE

UK	US
4 ply	Sport
Double Knitting	Light Worsted
Aran	Fisherman/Worsted
Chunky	Bulky
Super Chunky	Extra Bulky

KNITTING NEEDLE CONVERSION TABLE

Metric	UK	US
2 mm	14	0
2.25 mm	13	1
2.75 mm	12	2
3 mm	11	2 or3
3.25 mm	10	3
3.75 mm	9	5
4 mm	8	6
4.5 mm	7	7
5 mm	6	8
5.5 mm	5	9
6 mm	4	10
6.5 mm	3	10½
7 mm	2	10½
7.5 mm	1	11
8 mm	0	11
9 mm	00	13
10 mm	000	15

YARNS

Throughout this chapter, where possible, double knitting yarns have been used so that colour changes can be made very easily. Always bear in mind the child for which the toy is intended, and alter the skin tone, hair colour and clothes accordingly. Any child will delight in a truly individual toy made specifically for them.

Please do experiment with different colourways and combinations. Be sure to knit a tension square to make sure you are happy with the effect it may produce. Also, it is always best to substitute yarns with a similar meterage/yardage, so that the resulting toy is as close as possible to the original design.

Please note: some of the toys have 100 g balls listed in the requirements, this is because the yarn is only available in that weight of ball but the toy will not use all of the yarn. Therefore, if you do use a substitute yarn, you may only need a fraction of 100 g.

ABBREVIATIONS

The following are the general abbreviations used in the patterns:

alt	alternate
beg	begin(ning)
ch	chain stitch (crochet)
cm	centimetres
cont	continu(e)(ing)
dc	double crochet
dec	decreas(e)(ing)
foll	following
g st	garter stitch (k every row)
in	inch(es)
inc	increase(e)(ing)
k	knit
m1	make one, by picking up the bar between last stitch and the next and working into the back of it
meas	measures
mm	millimetre(s)
p	purl
patt	pattern
psso	pass slipped stitch over
rem	remain(ing)
rep	repeat(s)(ing)
rev st st	reverse stocking stitch
RS	right side
skpo	slip 1, knit 1, pass slipped stitch over
sl 1	slip 1 stitch
ss	slip stich (crochet)
st(s)	stitch(es)
st st	stocking stitch (RS row k, WS row p)
tbl	through back of loop(s)
tog	together
tr	treble
WS	wrong side
yb	yarn back
yfwd	yarn forward
yon	yarn over needle
yrn	yarn round needle
[ ]	work instructions inside [ ]s as many times as instructed
*	repeat instructions between asterisks as many times as instructed

KNITTED FABRICS

All knitted fabrics are made using just two basic stitches, knit and purl.

1 GARTER STITCH (g st)
This is when every row is knitted in the same stitch, either knit every row, or purl every row. This produces a reversible fabric with horizontal ridges that does not curl at the edges.

2 STOCKING STITCH (st st)
This is the most widely used knitted fabric. Alternate rows are knitted, the others are purled. With the knit side as the right side, the fabric is smooth and flat.

With the purl side as the right side (referred to as reverse stocking stitch) the fabric has horizontal ridges, which are closer together than in garter stitch. Stocking stitch will curl at the edges and, therefore, needs borders or seams to keep it flat.

3 MOSS STITCH (moss st)
This is a textured stitch made up of alternate knit and purl stitches. Stitches that are knitted on one row will be knitted again on the next row.

Stitches that are purled on one row will, again, be purled on the next. This produces a reversible, textured fabric that does not curl at the edges.

TENSION

For each pattern there is a recommended tension/gauge. It can seem like a chore to have to knit a tension square, but it is extremely important as it can make the difference between a great looking toy that is perfect in size and shape, and one that is disappointing. The tension for the plain knitted toys needs to be fairly tight to result in a firm fabric that can be stuffed well. Too loose a tension will result in an open fabric through which stuffing will show. Too tight a tension will result in a stiff looking toy without much pliability.

Before starting a project, knit a tension square 5–10 more stitches and 5–10 more rows than stated in the tension note. Lay the finished square on a flat surface and smooth out, taking care not to distort the stitches. Use a ruler or metal tape measure to measure a 10 cm (4 in) square. Using pins as markers, pin vertically between stitches and horizontally between rows. Count the number of stitches and rows between the markers. If you have more stitches and rows than is stated in the tension note, you are knitting too tightly and you will need to try again with needles that are one size larger. If you have too few stitches and rows you are knitting too loosely and you will need to try again with needles that are one size smaller. Once you have achieved the correct tension your toy will be knitted to the measurements given at the beginning of each pattern.

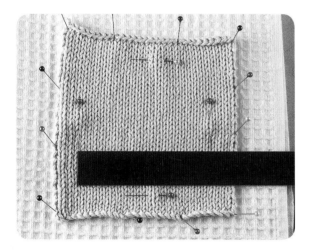

BASIC SHAPING

All of the projects in this book contain basic shaping techniques. Shaping is achieved by increasing and decreasing during knitting to form the fabric into the required shape. The methods I have used are described below.

INCREASING THE NUMBER OF STITCHES IN A ROW

MAKE ONE (M1): pick up the horizontal bar in between this stitch and the next with your right needle. Place it onto your left needle and then knit into the back loop.

INCREASE KNIT WISE (INC): knit into the front loop of the stitch as normal but do not slip the stitch off the left needle. Instead knit into the back loop of the same stitch.

DECREASING THE NUMBER OF STITCHES IN A ROW

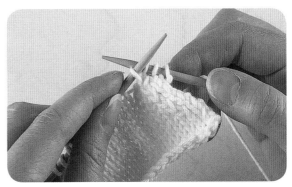

SKPO: slip one stitch without knitting it onto your right needle, knit one stitch then, using the point of the left needle, lift the slipped stitch over the knitted stitch.

K2 TOG: place the point of the right needle into the front loops of the first two stitches on the left needle and knit both loops at the same time.

COLOUR KNITTING

There are two main methods of working different colours in knitted fabric: intarsia and fairisle. The intarsia technique is usually used where a block of colour is required in just one area of the row, and there is usually a chart to follow for this. The fairisle technique is used when a pattern is repeated across the row, working different colours a few stitches at a time.

INTARSIA

For the intarsia technique it is best to have small lengths, balls or bobbins of yarn for each area of colour along the row. This produces a single thickness of fabric and the yarn is not carried across the back of the knitting so that the motif does not become distorted. Join in the various colours at the appropriate point in the row, and to avoid gaps in the knitting as you change colour, twist the yarns around each other on the wrong side. All ends can then be darned in at the end or knitted in as you work.

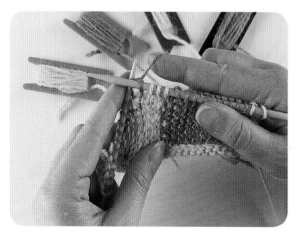

CHARTS

Some of the patterns in the book contain charts for intarsia knitting. Each square on the chart represents one stitch and each line of squares represents one row of knitting. When working from the charts, read odd rows (K) from right to left, and even rows (P) from left to right. Each colour used is given a different symbol and these are shown in the key alongside each chart.

MAKING UP AND FINISHING

Please spend time finishing and making up the finished item neatly, as although the process can be time consuming, the resulting toy will be a professional looking one.

PRESSING

When you have finished knitting all the pieces of your toy, sew in all the yarn ends neatly.

Most of the shaped pieces, and those using acrylic yarns, are best not pressed. Any lumps and bumps should be smoothed away when the toy is stuffed. However, any garments would benefit from being blocked and pressed lightly beneath a dry cloth to aid making up. Please refer to ball band instructions if you are at all unsure about pressing.

BACK STITCH

Unless otherwise stated, back stitch is good for sewing up the majority of the toys. With stripes and patterns, make sure to match the edges well.

Place the two pieces of knitting right sides together and pin in place. Thread a length of the correct coloured yarn into a large-eyed, darning needle and secure it to the knitting where you want to begin stitching. Bring the needle up through both pieces of knitting, to the front one row up from the bottom of the knitting. Take the needle back down to the bottom edge and insert it, then bring it back up two rows up from the bottom edge. Insert back in at the top of the first stitch and then back out two rows up. Continue in this way so that every stitch is one row down and

two rows up, until the end of the seam. Fasten off. Use the ridges and lines of the knitting to guide you so that your seams are kept straight.

MATTRESS STITCH

Use mattress stitch to join centre back body and leg seams and any other seam where you want a particularly neat finish, as it produces a virtually invisible seam.

Thread a length of the correct coloured yarn into a large eyed, darning needle and secure it to one piece of knitting where you want to begin stitching. Bring the needle to the front between the first and second stitches. Now arrange both pieces of knitting to be joined with right sides facing you. Insert the needle between the first two stitches on the other piece and then again on the first piece. Keep stitching in this way, forming a neat zig zag of stitches between the two pieces and pulling the knitted pieces together every few stitches, until you reach the end of the seam. Fasten off.

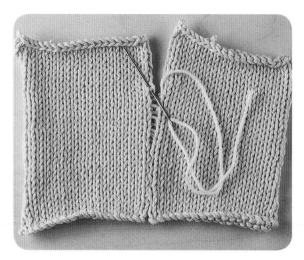

STUFFING

Always use washable toy stuffing that conforms to all safety regulations to stuff your toys. The golden rule with stuffing is; moderation. Overstuffing will distort the fabric and make the toy stiff, board-like and heavy. Understuffing will result in a limp-looking toy.

EMBROIDERY STITCHES

Stranded embroidery thread has been used to provide fine detail and definition to the features of all the toys. The following are the main embroidery stitches used.

STEM STITCH

This is mainly used for mouths and noses.

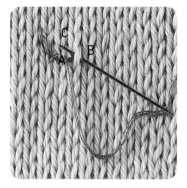

Bring needle out at A, insert back at B and emerge at C (half-way between A and B). Continue in this way, making short, slightly angled, and overlapping stitches, working from left to right.

SATIN STITCH

Mainly used for eyes, noses and nostrils. Bring the needle out at A and insert at B. Continue in this way working across the area to be covered either straight across or at an angle, making sure not to pull the stitches too tight and keep-ing neat edges to the stitched area. It sometimes helps to work a

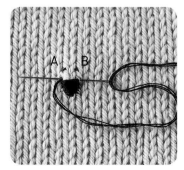

line of chain stitches or running stitches around the area to be filled with satin stitch, so that the edges remain neat.

ADDITIONAL TECHNIQUES
Some of the toys have scarves and hats that require fringing and pom poms.

FRINGING
Cut the yarn to the required lengths. With the wrong side of the knitted fabric facing you, insert a crochet hook from the front to the back. Fold the yarn in half, place the loop on the hook and pull the loop of yarn through. Thread the ends of yarn through the loop and pull to make a knot against the edge of the knitted fabric. Continue as per the instructions given for that particular toy's scarf.

POM-POMS
To make pom-poms it is easiest to use one of the kits that are readily available. The kits usually contain plastic semi-circles that clip together and allow you to wind your chosen yarn around. You then cut the yarn and remove the plastic parts to use again. Alternatively, you can use cardboard circles and make pom-poms in the conventional way.

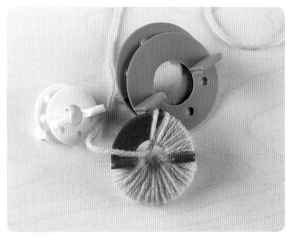

Felting Information

YARNS

Most 100 per cent wool, alpaca, mohair or animal fibre blends will felt well. However, it is best to avoid any 100 per cent wool yarns that are labelled "machine washable" or "superwash" as these have been chemically treated so that the fibres will not burst or matt, however roughly they are treated. Also, certain colours, in particular heather mixtures, felt much less quickly than others.

Some of the toys in this chapter have been made from knitting that has been felted. Traditionally, the term "felting" is only applied to raw, carded wool which is washed with soap and water to form a fluffy, matted fabric. When the same process is applied to knitted fabric it is called "fulling". The combination of hot and cold water, soap and agitation causes the fibres in the yarn to fluff, burst and matt slightly. Fulled fabric, therefore, is more dense, soft and warm to wear as it is less penetrable than ordinary knitted fabric. For the purposes of this chapter, however, I shall continue to refer to the process as felting.

TENSION

For all of the felted toys you will notice that the knitted tension is deliberately loose. This is to allow for the shrinkage that will occur when the knitting is felted. Most knitted pieces will shrink much more in length than in width and this has been accounted for.

I cannot stress enough the importance of tension swatch knitting, especially as the knitting is going to be felted.

I know it can seem like a chore to have to knit and then felt a tension swatch, when you've got your heart set on knitting that cute, felted chap, but it can save you from some very costly mistakes. I know the disastrous results that can be had from not testing tension swatches in my washing machine.

When you knit a tension square for felting, it is a good idea to mark the 10 cm (4 in) square area with markers made from a yarn that will not

felt (e.g. cotton). In this way, after washing, you will clearly be able to see how much shrinkage has occurred over the area without having to try and count stitches and rows that have become blurred by felting.

Try experimenting with any oddments of 100 per cent wool, or wool blend, yarns that you have and see what results you get. Make sure to make notes on everything you do so that you can work out the shrinkage and repeat the process for a toy.

Above: Tension swatches showing before felting (left) and after felting (right). Note the pink yarn markers.

METHOD

There are two main ways of felting knitted fabric; either by hand or in the washing machine. FELTING BY HAND allows you to control the level to which your knitting is felted and therefore, allows you to stop when you reach the desired level. FELTING BY MACHINE, while producing good results in the main, is more variable as different makes of washing machine vary so greatly. Also, you only see the results at the end of the wash cycle by which time it may be too late! If you have a top loading washing machine, you may find machine felting much easier. You are able to periodically stop the wash cycle and fish out your knitted pieces to check on their progress, continuing until you are happy with the results.

Most of the toys in this chapter have been felted by hand, but the following instructions include both methods.

HOW TO FELT KNITTING IN THE WASHING MACHINE

Materials and Tools

• knitted pieces with all the ends sewn in
• soap rather than detergent, it can be liquid or flakes but look for 'soap' on the label
• jeans or an item of clothing that will withstand being washed at 60°C (not towels as the lint transfers)
• washing machine
• towel for drying

1 Place the knitted pieces in the washing machine with the jeans (this aids the agitation), and the soap, and wash on a 60°C wash cycle.

2 When the cycle has finished, remove the knitted pieces and gently tease the matted edges apart, and reshape.

3 Squeeze out any excess water by rolling the pieces in a towel.

4 Dry supported on a towel, out of direct sunlight.

HOW TO FELT KNITTING BY HAND

Materials and Tools

• knitted pieces with all the ends sewn in
• soap rather than detergent, it can be liquid or flakes, but look for 'soap' on the label
• two large shallow bowls (or sink and a large bowl)
• pair of thick rubber gloves
• hot and cold water
• ice cubes
• towel for drying

1 Fill the sink, or one bowl, with just boiled water and, wearing the rubber gloves, carefully add a handful of soap flakes or liquid and stir. Place the knitted pieces in the water and, making sure they're completely covered, leave to soak for a few minutes.

2 Meanwhile, fill the other bowl with cold water and ice cubes.

3 Begin to knead, rub and agitate the knitted pieces vigorously in the hot water, taking care not to scald yourself.

4 Then switch to the cold water bowl and continue rubbing and agitating. Felting may happen quickly, or it may take several switches between the hot and the cold water.

5 Make sure to rub the piece evenly all over to retain the shape. Cords can be rolled between the hands to encourage felting.

6 Keep the temperature of each bowl of water to its optimum level so that the knitting felts quickly.

7 When you have achieved your desired level of felting, rinse the pieces well. Squeeze out any excess water by rolling the pieces in a towel.

8 Dry supported on a towel, out of direct sunlight.

Timings

Each pattern states how long, and which method of felting, is required. The figure represents the total time spent on the process, felting all the pieces for that toy together.

I prefer a lightly felted appearance to retain a little stitch definition. However, if you prefer a more felted look, then continue with the process until you reach the desired level. Please be aware that the more you felt the pieces the thicker they will become and the smaller the resulting toy will be.

Ziggy Zebra

Ziggy is approximately 35 cm (14 in) tall.

MATERIALS

- 2 x 25 g balls of Shetland Wool Brokers 2 ply Jumper Weight in Navy 21
- 2 x 25 g balls of Shetland Wool Brokers 2 ply Jumper Weight in Pale Blue 14
- pair of 5.5 mm (UK 5/US 9) knitting needles
- stranded embroidery thread in Black and White
- washable toy stuffing

TENSION

16 sts and 23 rows to 10 cm (4 in) measured over stocking stitch using 5.5 mm (UK 5/US 9) needles and 2 strands of yarn, before hand felting.

Note: Two strands of yarn are used together, throughout, for all pieces.

Navy and pale blue stripes offer a twist on traditional zebra colours in this knitted version. Ziggy is bound to become a firm favourite with your little one.

BODY FRONT

With 5.5 mm (UK 5/US 9) needles and 2 strands of Navy, cast on 19 sts.
Beg with a k row and working 2 rows Navy, 2 rows Pale Blue throughout, work 26 rows in st st.
* **Next row**: K1, skpo, k to last 3 sts, k2tog, k1.
P 1 row.
Rep last 2 rows once more (15 sts).
Cast off. *

BODY BACK

With 5.5 mm (UK 5/US 9) needles and 2 strands of Navy, cast on 19 sts.
Beg with a k row, work 2 rows in st st.
SHAPE BASE
Next row: Sl 1, yf, sl 1, yb, k to last 2 sts, yf, sl 1, yb, sl 1.
P 1 row.

Rep the last 2 rows twice more.
Change to Pale Blue. Beg with a k row and working 2 rows Pale Blue, 2 rows Navy throughout, work 20 rows in st st.
Work as for body front from * to *.

ARMS (make 2)

With 5.5 mm (UK 5/US 9) needles and 2 strands of Pale Blue, cast on 15 sts.
Beg with a k row and working 2 rows Pale Blue, 2 rows Navy throughout, work 18 rows in st st.
Beg with a k row and working in Navy only, work 4 rows in st st.
Next row: K1, skpo, k3, skpo, k4, k2tog, k1 (12 sts)
P 1 row.
Next row: K1, [k2tog] 5 times, k1 (7 sts).
P 1 row.
Cast off.

LEGS (make 2)

With 5.5 mm (UK 5/US 9) needles and 2 strands of Navy, cast on 20 sts.
Beg with a k row work 6 rows in st st.
Change to Pale Blue. Beg with a k row and working 2 rows Pale Blue, 2 rows Navy throughout, work 24 rows in st st.
Cast off.

LEG BASES (make 2)

With 5.5 mm (UK 5/US 9) needles and 2 strands of Navy, cast on 4 sts.
Next row: Inc 1 st at each end of row.
P 1 row.

Rep the last 2 rows once more (8 sts).
Next row: Dec 1 st at each end of row.
P 1 row.
Rep the last 2 rows once more (4 sts).
Cast off.

HEAD

With 5.5 mm (UK 5/US 9) needles and 2 strands of Navy, cast on 15 sts.
K 1 row.
Next row: [P1, m1] to last 2 sts, p2 (28 sts).
Change to Pale Blue.
Next row: K8, [m1, k2] 6 times, m1, k8 (35 sts).
P 1 row.
Cont in 2 rows Navy, 2 rows Pale Blue throughout, work 6 rows in st st.
Next row: K8, skpo, k3, skpo, k1, skpo, k1, k2tog, k3, k2tog, k9 (30 sts).
Beg with a p row, and cont in 2 row stripes, work 11 rows in st st.
Next row: K8, [skpo] twice, k6, [k2tog] twice, k8 (26 sts).
P 1 row.
Cast off.

MUZZLE

With 5.5 mm (UK 5/US 9) needles and 2 strands of Pale Blue, cast on 30 sts.
Beg with a k row, work 6 rows in st st.
Next row: K7, [skpo] twice, k8, [k2tog] twice, k7 (26 sts).
P 1 row.
Next row: K5, [skpo] 3 times, k4, [k2tog] 3 times, k5 (20 sts).

P 1 row.
Next row: K1, [k2tog] to last st, k1 (11 sts).
P 1 row.
Cast off.

EARS (make 2)
With 5.5 mm (UK 5/US 9) needles and 2 strands of
Pale Blue, cast on 5 sts.
Beg with a k row, work 4 rows in st st.
Next row: Skpo, k1, k2tog (3 sts).
Change to Navy.
P 1 row.
Next row: [K1, m1] twice, k1 (5 sts).
Beg with a p row, work 7 rows in st st.
Cast off.

TAIL
With 5.5 mm (UK 5/US 9) needles and 2 strands of
Navy, cast on 3 sts.
K 1 row, turn and sl all sts back onto the right
needle.
Turn again, and pulling the yarn tight from the left
side, k across the 3 sts. In this way you will k all
rows and the row ends will pull together to make
a tube.
Cont in this way until the tail measures 10 cm
(4 in).
Cast off.
Loop 6 lengths of Navy yarn, each 8 cm (3 in),
through one end of the tail.

FELTING INSTRUCTIONS

Work in all ends with a needle.
Following the instructions in the felting
techniques section for hand felting, felt all pieces
for approximately 20 minutes.
Reshape while damp, and dry thoroughly.

TO MAKE UP

Join each inside leg seam and stitch to each
leg base. Stuff firmly and oversew cast-off
edges together.
Sew underarm seam of each arm and stuff firmly.
Oversew cast-on edges together.
Pin oversewn edges of legs to lower front body
and one arm to side of front body. Sew front body
to back body through all thicknesses, leaving one
side open. Turn to right side, attach other arm
and close side seam.
Stuff firmly and close top seam.
Sew tail to centre of broad Navy section on back
body.
Sew centre back seam of head.
Fold each ear in half and sew row ends together.
Pin ears inside top seam of head and sew through
all thicknesses to close.
Stuff head firmly.
Join seam of muzzle and stuff. Sew muzzle to
front of head, positioning over shaping.
Sew head to shoulders.
Stitch eyes and nostrils in satin stitch using
black embroidery thread. Work mouth in black
embroidery thread using stem stitch. Sew a small
white highlight in each eye.

Dylan Donkey

Dylan Donkey is approximately 35 cm (14 in) tall.

A soft, cuddly friend, with cute tufts of hair; Dylan Donkey is sure to become a firm favourite with your special little person.

MATERIALS
- 1 x 100 g ball of pure wool chunky in Grey
- 1 x 100 g ball of pure wool chunky in White
- pair of 8 mm (UK 0/US 11) knitting needles
- stranded embroidery thread in Black and White
- Washable toy stuffing

TENSION
11 sts and 15 rows to 10 cm (4 in) measured over stocking stitch using 8 mm (UK 0/US 11) needles before machine felting.

BODY (make 2)
With 8 mm (UK 0/US 11) needles and Grey, cast on 14 sts.
Beg with a k row, work 4 rows in st st.
Next row: Inc 1 st at each end of row (16 sts).
Beg with a p row, work 9 rows in st st.
Beg with a k row, work 14 rows in st st, at the same time, dec 1 st at each end of every 3rd row (8 sts).
Cast off.

HEAD
With 8 mm (UK 0/US 11) needles and Grey, cast on 12 sts.
Beg with a k row, work 2 rows in st st.
Next row: Inc 1 st k wise in every st (24 sts).
P 1 row.
Next row: K6, [m1, k2] 6 times, m1, k6 (31 sts).
Beg with a p row, work 5 rows in st st.

BODY (make 2)

With 8 mm (UK 0/US 11) needles and Grey, cast on 14 sts.
Beg with a k row, work 4 rows in st st.
Next row: Inc 1 st at each end of row (16 sts).
Beg with a p row, work 9 rows in st st.
Beg with a k row, work 14 rows in st st, at the same time, dec 1 st at each end of every 3rd row (8 sts).
Cast off.

HEAD

With 8 mm (UK 0/US 11) needles and Grey, cast on 12 sts.
Beg with a k row, work 2 rows in st st.
Next row: Inc 1 st k wise in every st (24 sts).
P 1 row.
Next row: K6, [m1, k2] 6 times, m1, k6 (31 sts).
Beg with a p row, work 5 rows in st st.
Next row: K6, [k2tog, k1] 6 times, k2tog, k5 (24 sts).
Beg with a p row, work 7 rows in st st.
Next row: [K2tog] to end (12 sts).
P 1 row.
Cast off.

MUZZLE

With 8 mm (UK 0/US 11) needles and White, cast on 24 sts.
Beg with a k row, work 6 rows in st st.
Next row: K3, [k2tog, k2] to last 5 sts, k2tog, k3 (19 sts).
P 1 row.
Next row: K1, [k2tog] to end (10 sts).

P 1 row.
Cast off.

BODY (make 2)

With 8 mm (UK 0/US 11) needles and Grey, cast on 14 sts.
Beg with a k row, work 4 rows in st st.
Next row: Inc 1 st at each end of row (16 sts).
Beg with a p row, work 9 rows in st st.
Beg with a k row, work 14 rows in st st, at the same time, dec 1 st at each end of every 3rd row. (8 sts.)
Cast off.

HEAD

With 8 mm (UK 0/US 11) needles and Grey, cast on 12 sts.
Beg with a k row, work 2 rows in st st.
Next row: Inc 1 st k wise in every st (24 sts).
P 1 row.
Next row: K6, [m1, k2] 6 times, m1, k6 (31 sts).
Beg with a p row, work 5 rows in st st.
Next row: K6, [k2tog, k1] 6 times, k2tog, k5 (24 sts).
Beg with a p row, work 7 rows in st st.
Next row: [K2tog] to end (12 sts).
P 1 row.
Cast off.

MUZZLE

With 8 mm (UK 0/US 11) needles and White, cast on 24 sts.
Beg with a k row, work 6 rows in st st.
Next row: K3, [k2tog, k2] to last 5 sts, k2tog, k3

(19 sts).
P 1 row.
Next row: K1, [k2tog] to end (10 sts).
P 1 row.
Cast off.

EARS (make 2 Grey, 2 White)
With 8 mm (UK 0/US 11) needles and Grey, cast on 3 sts.
Beg with a k row, work 4 rows in st st.
Next row: K2tog, k1.
Next row: P2tog.
Break yarn, thread through rem st, pull tightly and fasten off.

LEGS (Make 2)
With 8 mm (UK 0/US 11) needles and White, cast on 15 sts.
Beg with a k row, work 4 rows in st st.
Change to Grey and beg with a k row, work 12 rows in st st.
Cast off.

LEG BASES (make 2)
With 8 mm (UK 0/US 11) needles and White, cast on 4 sts.
Beg with a k row, work 2 rows in st st.
Next row: Inc 1 st at each end of row (6 sts).
P 1 row.
Next row: K2tog, k2, k2tog (4 sts).
P 1 row.
Cast off.

ARMS (make 2)
With 8 mm (UK 0/US 11) needles and White, cast on 12 sts.
Beg with a k row, work 4 rows in st st.
Change to Grey and beg with a k row, work 8 rows in st st.
Cast off 2 sts at beg of next 2 rows (8 sts).
Beg with a k row, work 3 rows in st st, at the same time dec 1 st at each end of every row (2 sts).
P 1 row.
Cast off.

ARM ENDS (make 2)
With 8 mm (UK 0/US 11) needles and White, cast on 2 sts.
Beg with a k row, work 2 rows in st st.
Next row: Inc 1 st in each st (4 sts).
P1 row.
Next row: [K2tog] twice (2 sts).
P 1 row.
Cast off.

FELTING INSTRUCTIONS
Work in all ends with a needle.
HAIR: Before felting; take 10 lengths each 8 cm (3 in) of Grey yarn and, following the fringing instructions, loop one length through each stitch of the cast-off edge of the head, ignoring the first and last stitch, and form a knot.
Following the instructions in the felting techniques section for machine felting, felt all pieces in the washing machine on a 60°C wash. Reshape while damp, and dry thoroughly.

TO MAKE UP

Join side seams of body.

Sew leg seams and then sew leg bases into each leg. Stuff firmly, then oversew the top edges, gathering slightly.

Place the oversewn ends of the legs into the bottom opening of the body, and sew through all thicknesses. Stuff body firmly and close top opening.

Sew centre back seam of head. Sew top of head together on right side, so that the tufts of hair are visible. Stuff head. Close seam at bottom of head. Sew muzzle seam. Stuff and sew to front of head over shaping.

Sew one White and one Grey ear together for each ear. Then sew ears to head at each side of hair tufts.

Sew head to body.

Sew arm seams, then sew an end into each arm. Stuff firmly and sew to sides of body.

Embroider eyes and nostrils in satin stitch using black embroidery thread. Outline each eye with white embroidery thread. Sew a small white highlight in each eye.

Cool Cat

Cool Cat is approximately 28 cm (11 in) tall.

Knitted in a wonderful tweed yarn that felts beautifully, here's a cuddly, cool cat waiting to be a cute companion.

MATERIALS

- 2 x 25 g balls of Shade 125 Jamieson & Smith 2 ply jumper weight
- 1 x 25 g ball of Shade 072 Jamieson & Smith 2 ply jumper weight
- 1 x 25 g ball of Shade FC38 Jamieson & Smith 2 ply jumper weight
- 1 x 25 g ball of Shade 080 Jamieson & Smith 2 ply jumper weight
- pair of 5.5 mm (UK 5/US 9) knitting needles
- stranded embroidery thread in Black and White
- washable toy stuffing

TENSION

16 sts and 22 rows to 10 cm (4 in) measured over stocking stitch using 5.5 mm (UK 5/US 9) needles and 2 strands of yarn, before hand felting.

Note: Two strands of yarn are used together, throughout, for all pieces.

BODY

RIGHT LEG

* With 5.5 mm (UK 5/US 9) needles and 2 strands of Orange, cast on 10 sts.
Next row: Inc 1 st, k wise, in every st (20 sts).
Beg with a p row, work 19 rows in st st.*
Break yarn and place sts on a spare needle.

LEFT LEG

Work as for right leg from * to *.
Join legs
With RS facing and 2 strands of Dark Red, k across 20 sts of left leg, then 20 sts of right leg (40 sts).
Next row: P20, m1, p20 (41 sts).
Beg with a k row and working 2 rows Orange, 2 rows Light Brown, 2 rows Dark Brown and 2 rows Dark Red throughout, work 28 rows in st st.

Shape shoulders
Cont stripe sequence as set, work as follows:
Next row: K9, skpo, k19, k2tog, k9 (39 sts).
P 1 row.
Next row: K2, [k2tog, k1] to last 4 sts, k2tog, k2
(27 sts).
P 1 row.
Cast off.

HEAD (make 2)
With 5.5 mm (UK 5/US 9) needles and 2 strands of
Orange, cast on 6 sts.
K 1 row.
Cast on 2 sts at beg of next 4 rows (14 sts).
P 1 row.
Inc 1 st at each end of next and foll alt row
(18 sts).
Beg with a p row, work 11 rows in st st.
Divide for ears
Next row: K5, cast off 8 sts, k5.
Working on these 5 sts only as follows:
Next row: P3, p2tog (4 sts).
Next row: K2tog, k2 (3 sts).
Next row: P1, p2tog (2 sts).
Next row: K2tog.
Break yarn, thread through rem st and fasten off.
With WS facing, rejoin yarn to rem 5 sts and work
as for first ear, reversing all shapings.

ARMS (make 2)
With 5.5 mm (UK 5/US 9) needles and 2 strands of
Orange, cast on 8 sts.
Next row: Inc 1 st, k wise, in every st (16 sts).
Beg with a p row, work 19 rows in st st.

Shape top
Beg with a k row, work 6 rows in st st, dec 1 st at
each end of every row (4 sts).
Cast off.

TAIL
With 5.5 mm (UK 5/US 9) needles and 2 strands of
Orange, cast on 4 sts.
K 1 row, turn and sl all sts back onto the right
needle.
Turn again, and pulling the yarn tight from the
left side, k across the 4 sts. In this way you will
k all rows and the row-ends will pull together to
make a tube.

Cont in this way until the tail measures 10 cm (4 in).
Break yarn, thread through sts, draw up tightly and fasten off.

FELTING INSTRUCTIONS
Work in all ends with a needle.
Following the instructions in the felting techniques section for hand felting, felt all pieces for approximately 25 minutes.
Reshape while damp, and dry thoroughly.

TO MAKE UP
Sew each inside leg seam. Then sew the centre back seam catching the tail into the seam just above the tops of the legs. Stuff and close top opening.
With right sides together, sew the two head pieces together, leaving an opening. Turn to right side, stuff firmly and close opening.
Sew head to body.
Sew bottom and underarm seam of each arm. Stuff and sew to sides of body.
Work eyes and nose in satin stitch using black embroidery thread. Work mouth and whiskers in stem stitch and black embroidery thread. Sew a small white highlight in each eye.
Using black embroidery thread, work 'claws' on hands and feet in stem stitch.

Stripes the Tiger

Stripes the Tiger is approximately 28 cm (11 in) long.

MATERIALS

- •1 x 50 g ball of 100 per cent alpaca DK in Orange
- • 1 x 50 g ball of 100 per cent alpaca in Black
- • pair of 4.5 mm (UK 7/US 7) knitting needles
- • stranded embroidery thread in Black and White
- • washable toy stuffing

TENSION

20 sts and 25 rows to 10 cm (4 in) measured over stocking stitch using 4.5 mm (UK 7/US 7) needles before hand felting.

> A little jungle friend for your wild one! This striped tiger would look wonderful lying on a child's bed, and the 100 per cent Alpaca yarn is lovely to cuddle up to.

BODY

FIRST FRONT LEG

* With 4.5 mm (UK 7/US 7) needles and Orange, cast on 19 sts.
Beg with a k row, work 2 rows in st st.

Next row: K1, m1, k8, m1, k1, m1, k8, m1, k1 (23 sts).
Beg with a p row, work 7 rows in st st.
Change to Black, and working in stripes of 2 rows Black, 4 rows Orange throughout, cont as follows:
Beg with a k row, work 10 rows in st st. *
Break yarn and place sts on a spare needle.

SECOND FRONT LEG

Work as first front leg from * to *.

Join legs

With 4.5 mm (UK 7/US 7) needles and Orange, and RS facing, k across 23 sts of second front leg, then 23 sts of first front leg (46 sts).
Next row: P22, [m1, p1] 3 times, p21 (49 sts).
Change to Black and stripe sequence as set, beg with a k row, work 40 rows in st st.

Divide for back legs

Next row: K23, cast off 3 sts, k to end.

FIRST BACK LEG

** Working on these 23 sts, and stripe sequence as set, cont as follows:

Beg with a p row, work 9 rows in st st.

Change to Orange, cont in Orange only, and beg with a k row, work 8 rows in st st.

Next row: K1, k2tog, k7, [k2tog] twice, k6, k2tog, k1 (19 sts).

P 1 row.

Cast off. **

SECOND BACK LEG

With WS facing, rejoin yarn to rem sts and rep from ** to **.

HEAD (make 2)

With 4.5 mm (UK 7/US 7) needles and Orange, cast on 8 sts.

Working in stripes of 4 rows Orange, 2 rows Black, cont as follows.

Beg with a k row, work 2 rows in st st.

Cast on 2 sts at beg of next 7 rows (22 sts).

Beg with a p row, work 13 rows in st st.

Shape ears

Next row: K5, cast off 12 sts, k5.

FIRST EAR

Work on these 5 sts only and stripe sequence, cont as follows:

P 1 row.

Next row: K2tog, k to end (4 sts).

Next row: P2, p2tog (3 sts).

Next row: K2tog, k1 (2 sts).

Next row: P2tog.

Break yarn, thread through rem st, draw up tightly and fasten off.

SECOND EAR

With WS facing, rejoin yarn to rem sts and work as for first ear, reversing all shaping.

FACE

With 4.5 mm (UK 7/US 7) needles and Orange, cast on 7 sts.

Beg with a k row, work 2 rows in st st.

Then, beg with a k row, work 4 rows in st st, inc 1 st at each end of every row (15 sts).

Now, beg with a k row, work 6 rows in st st.

Next row: K2tog, k4, k2tog, turn (6 sts).

Next row: P2tog, p2, p2tog (4 sts).

Cast off.

With RS facing, rejoin yarn to rem 7 sts and work as follows:

Next row: K2tog, k to end (6 sts).

Next row: P2tog, p2, p2tog (4 sts).

Cast off.

TAIL

With 4.5 mm (UK 7/US 7) needles and Orange, cast on 7 sts.

Beg with a k row and working stripes of 4 rows Orange, 2 rows Black, work 22 rows in st st. Cast off.

FELTING INSTRUCTIONS

Work in all ends with a needle.

Following the instructions in the felting techniques section for hand felting, felt all pieces for approximately 30 minutes.

Reshape while damp, and dry thoroughly.

TO MAKE UP

Sew each inside leg seam, then the centre body seam, leaving an opening for stuffing.

Stuff legs and body firmly and close opening.

Fold tail in half lengthways and join one end and long seam. Stuff lightly. Sew to back just above back legs.

Sew head pieces together, leaving an opening for stuffing. Stuff firmly and close opening. Sew face to front head. Sew head to body.

Embroider eyes and nose in satin stitch using black embroidery thread. Embroider mouth in stem stitch using black. Sew a small white highlight in each eye.

Sew 'claws' on each paw in stem stitch using black embroidery thread.

Maisie Moo

Maisie Moo is approximately 30 cm (12 in) tall.

> Who says that cows have to be black and white? This fun green and yellow version is sure to raise a smile in all who see her.

MATERIALS

- 2 x 50 g balls of 100 per cent Alpaca DK in Yellow
- 1 x 50 g ball of 100 per cent Alpaca DK in Green
- 1 x 50 g ball of 100 per cent Alpaca DK in Pink
- Pair of 4.5 mm (UK 7/US 7) knitting needles
- Stranded embroidery thread in Black and White
- Washable toy stuffing

TENSION

20 sts and 25 rows to 10 cm (4 in) measured over stocking stitch using 4.5 mm (UK 7/US 7) needles before hand felting.

BODY (make 2)
With 4.5 mm (UK 7/US 7) needles and Yellow, cast on 28 sts.
Beg with a k row, work 2 rows in st st.

Using the intarsia method, cont as follows:
Row 3: K1, m1, k4 Yellow, 13 Green, 9 Yellow, m1, k1 (30 sts).
Row 4: P11 Yellow, 13 Green, 6 Yellow.
Row 5: K6 Yellow, 12 Green, 12 Yellow.
Row 6: With Green, P1, m1, p3 Green, 8 Yellow, 11 Green, 6 Yellow, with Green m1, p1 (32 sts).
Row 7: K3 Green, 6 Yellow, 9 Green, 7 Yellow, 7 Green.
Row 8: P8 Green, 7 Yellow, 7 Green, 6 Yellow, 4 Green.
Row 9: K1, m1, k4 Green, 6 Yellow, 6 Green, 7 Yellow, 7 Green, m1, k1 (34 sts).
Row 10: P10 Green, 7 Yellow, 4 Green, 6 Yellow, 7 Green.
Row 11: K7 Green, 16 Yellow, 11 Green.
Row 12: P12 Green, 14 Yellow, 8 Green.
Row 13: K8 Green, 13 Yellow, 13 Green.

Row 14: P13 Green, 13 Yellow, 8 Green.
Row 15: K8 Green, 12 Yellow, 14 Green.
Row 16: P14 Green, 12 Yellow, 8 Green.
Row 17: As Row 15.
Row 18: As Row 16.
Row 19: K2tog, k6 Green, 13 Yellow, 11 Green, k2tog (32 sts).
Row 20: P11 Green, 14 Yellow, 7 Green.
Row 21: K7 Green, 14 Yellow, 11 Green.
Row 22: As Row 20.
Row 23: As Row 21.
Row 24: P10 Green, 5 Yellow, 3 Green, 7 Yellow, 7 Green.
Row 25: K6 Green, 7 Yellow, 5 Green, 4 Yellow, 10 Green.
Row 26: P9 Green, 5 Yellow, 6 Green, 6 Yellow, 6 Green.
Row 27: K2tog, k4 Green, 6 Yellow, 7 Green, 4 Yellow, 7 Green, k2tog (30 sts).
Row 28: P6 Green, 6 Yellow, 8 Green, 6 Yellow, 4 Green.
Row 29: K2 Green, 8 Yellow, 9 Green, 8 Yellow, 3 Green.
Row 30: With Yellow, p2tog, p9 Yellow, 9 Green, 8 Yellow, p2tog (28 sts).
Row 31: K9 Yellow, 9 Green, 10 Yellow.
Row 32: P10 Yellow, 9 Green, 9 Yellow.
Row 33: K2tog, k8 Yellow, 8 Green, 8 Yellow, k2tog (26 sts)
Row 34: P10 Yellow, 6 Green, 10 Yellow.
Row 35: K2tog, k9 Yellow, 4 Green, 9 Yellow, k2tog (24 sts).
Row 36: P all sts in Yellow.
Row 37: K2tog, k to last 2 sts, k2tog (22 sts).

Row 38: P2tog, p to last 2 sts, p2tog (20 sts).
K 1 row.
Row 40: P2tog, p to last 2 sts, p2tog (18 sts).
Beg with a k row, work 2 rows in st st.
Cast off.

BODY BASE
With 4.5 mm (UK 7/US 7) needles and Yellow, cast on 9 sts.
Beg with a k row, work 2 rows in st st.
Cast on 4 sts at beg of next 4 rows (25 sts).
Beg with a k row, work 2 rows in st st.
Cast off 4 sts at beg of next 4 rows (9 sts).
Beg with a k row, work 2 rows in st st.
Cast off.

ARMS (make 2)
With 4.5 mm (UK 7/US 7) needles and Yellow, cast on 19 sts.
Working from Chart A, work 22 rows in st st.
Cast off.

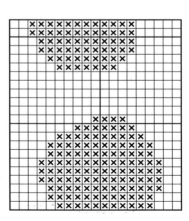

Key
☐ Yellow
☒ Green

Chart A

ARM HOOVES (make 2)

With 4.5 mm (UK 7/US 7) needles and Pink, cast on 7 sts.
Beg with a k row, work 8 rows in st st.
Cast off.

LEGS (make 2)

With 4.5 mm (UK 7/US 7) needles and Yellow, cast on 27 sts.
Working from Chart B, work 20 rows in st st.
Cast off.

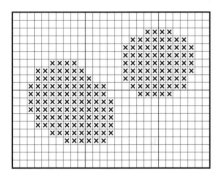

Chart B

LEG HOOVES (make 2)

With 4.5 mm (UK 7/US 7) needles and Pink, cast on 9 sts.
Beg with a k row, work 2 rows in st st.
Work 6 rows in st st, dec 1 st at each end of every alt row (3 sts).
Cast off.

HEAD

With 4.5 mm (UK 7/US 7) needles and Yellow, cast on 39 sts.
Beg with a k row, work 2 rows in st st.

Next row: K10, [m1, k2] 10 times, k9 (49 sts).
Beg with a p row, work 7 rows in st st.
Next row: K10, [k2tog, k1] 10 times, k9 (39 sts).
Beg with a p row, work 11 rows in st st.
Next row: K2, [k2tog, k1] to last 4 sts, k2tog, k2 (27 sts).
Next row: P1, [p2tog] to end (14 sts).
Cast off.

NOSE

With 4.5 mm (UK 7/US 7) needles and Pink, cast on 50 sts.
Beg with a k row, work 8 rows in st st.
Next row: K3, [k2tog, k4] to last 5 sts, k2tog, k3 (42 sts).
P 1 row.
Next row: K2, [k2tog, k3] to end (34 sts).
P 1 row.

Next row: K1, [k2tog, k1] to end (23 sts).
P 1 row.
Cast off.

EARS (make 2)

With 4.5 mm (UK 7/US 7) needles and Green, cast on 6 sts.
Beg with a k row, work 6 rows in st st.
Next row: Skpo, k2, k2tog (4 sts).
P 1 row.
Next row: K1, m1, k2, m1, k1 (6 sts).
Beg with a p row, work 7 rows in st st.
Cast off.

HORNS (make 2)

With 4.5 mm (UK 7/US 7) needles and Pink, cast on 8 sts.
Beg with a k row, work 6 rows in st st, at the same time dec 1 st at each end of every alt row (2 sts).
Work 2 rows in st st.
Cast off.

FELTING INSTRUCTIONS

Work in all ends with a needle.
Following the instructions in the felting techniques section for hand felting, felt all pieces for approximately 30 minutes.
Reshape while damp, and dry thoroughly.

TO MAKE UP

Stitch body pieces together at sides.
Sew leg seams. With cast-off edge of hoof to leg seam, sew hooves into cast-on ends of legs. Stuff and oversew ends.
Sew body base into bottom of body, sewing tops of legs into front of seam.
Stuff body and close seam.
Sew top and centre back seam of head and stuff.
Sew row-ends of nose together. With seam at centre, sew cast-off edges together. Stuff and sew to head over front shaping and bottom edges.
Sew horn seams and stuff. Oversew bottom edges. Sew row-ends of ears together and oversew bottom edges. Sew horns and ears to top of head.
Sew head to body.
Sew arm seams, then sew hooves in cast-off ends. Stuff, oversew ends then sew to sides of body.
Embroider eyes and nostrils in satin stitch using black embroidery thread. Sew a small white highlight in each eye.

Poppy Pig

Poppy Pig is approximately 25 cm (10 in) tall.

A sweet piglet knitted entirely in garter stitch makes for a wonderfully soft little friend. Her fun hat and scarf add to the cute effect.

Materials

- 2 x 50 g balls of Rowan Tweed in Hawes
- oddments of Bright Pink
- oddments of Green
- oddments of Blue
- pair of 4 mm (UK 8/US 6) knitting needles
- stranded embroidery thread in Black and White
- washable toy stuffing

Tension

30 sts and 21 rows to 10 cm (4 in) measured over garter stitch using 4 mm (UK 8/US 6) needles.

BODY FRONT

With 4 mm (UK 8/US 6) needles and Pink, cast on 34 sts.
*Work in g st throughout.
K 24 rows.
Then k 36 rows, at the same time, dec 1 st at each end of every foll 4th row * (16 sts).
Cast off.

BODY BACK

With 4 mm (UK 8/US 6) needles and Pink, cast on 36 sts.
Work as for Body Front from * to * (18 sts).
Cast off.

BODY BASE

With 4 mm (UK 8/US 6) needles and Pink, cast on 10 sts.
Work in g st throughout.
Cast on 2 sts at beg of next 2 rows (14 sts).

Inc 1 st at each end of next 7 rows (28 sts).
K 4 rows.
Dec 1 st at each end of next 7 rows (14 sts).
Cast off 2 sts at beg of next 2 rows (10 sts).
Cast off.

HEAD (make 2)

With 4 mm (UK 8/US 6) needles and Pink, cast on 5 sts.
Work in g st throughout.
Inc 1 st at each end of the next 4 rows (13 sts).
Now k 6 rows, inc 1 st at each end of every alt row (19 sts).
Then k 6 rows, inc 1 st at each end of every 3rd row (23 sts).
K 4 rows straight.
Now k 8 rows, inc 1 st at each end of every 4th row (27sts).
K 6 rows straight.
Then k 9 rows, dec 1 st at each end of every row (9 sts).
K 1 row.
Cast off.

SNOUT

With 4 mm (UK 8/US 6) needles and Pink, cast on 4 sts.
Work in g st throughout.
Cast on 2 sts at beg of next 2 rows (8 sts).
K 1 row.
Next row: Inc 1 st at each end of row (10 sts).
K 8 rows.
Next row: Dec 1 st at each end of row (8 sts).
K 1 row.

Cast off 2 sts at beg of next 2 rows (4 sts).
Cast off.

Snout side

With 4 mm (UK 8/US 6) needles and Pink, cast on 4 sts.
Work in g st throughout.
K until work measures 13 cm (5 in).
Cast off.

EARS (make 2)

With 4 mm (UK 8/US 6) needles and Pink, cast on 6 sts.
Work in g st throughout.
K 8 rows, inc 1 st at each end of every 4th row (10 sts).
K 4 rows.
Then k 4 rows, dec 1 st at each end of 4th row (8 sts).
K 6 rows, dec 1 st at each end of every alt row (2 sts).
K 1 row.
K2tog.
Break yarn and pull through rem st.

ARMS (make 2)

With 4 mm (UK 8/US 6) needles and Pink, cast on 4 sts.
K 2 rows.
Next row: K1, m1, k to last st, m1, k1 (6 sts).
K 1 row.
Rep the last 2 rows until there are 18 sts.
K 20 rows.
Next row: K1, [k2tog] to last st, k1 (10 sts).
Next row: [K2tog] 5 times (5 sts).

Break yarn, thread through rem 5 sts and draw up tightly.

LEGS (make 2)
With 4 mm (UK 8/US 6) needles and Pink, cast on 20 sts.
Work in g st throughout.
Next row: K4, m1, k to last 4 sts, m1, k4 (22 sts).
K 1 row.
Rep the last 2 rows until there are 38 sts.
K 4 rows straight.
Cast off.

HOOVES (make 2)
With 4 mm (UK 8/US 6) needles and Pink, cast on 4 sts.
Work in g st throughout.
K 2 rows.
Then k 12 rows, inc 1 st at each end of every 4th row (10 sts).
K 2 rows.
SHAPE TOES
Next row: K 5, turn.
Work on these sts only, as follows:
K 2 rows.
Next row: K2tog, k to end (4 sts).
K 1 row.
Next row: [K2tog] twice (2 sts).
K 1 row.
Cast off.
Rejoin yarn to rem sts and complete as for first toe, making first dec at inside edge of toe.

TAIL
With 4 mm (UK 8/US 6) needles and Pink, cast on 8 sts.
Next row: Inc k wise in every st (16 sts).
K 1 row.
Cast off loosely.

TO MAKE UP
Join side seams of body pieces. Sew body base to lower edges of body pieces. Stuff through top opening and then close seam. Fold each leg piece in half and sew short ends together. Sew each hoof into the broad end of each leg, lining up the

increase line with the points of the toes. Stuff lightly and oversew top edges together. Stitch to body placing oversewn edge on the seam line formed where the body meets the body base. Sew head pieces together catching in ears in the top seam and leaving an opening. Stuff and close opening. Sew head to body. Sew the cast-on and cast-off edges of the snout side together. Sew the snout side to the snout and stuff lightly. Sew to face. Catch the points of the ears forward onto the ears to form a fold. Sew each arm seam and stuff. Sew each arm to sides of body. Twist tail to form a spiral and stitch to back of body. Embroider eyes and nostrils in satin stitch, using black. Embroider mouth in stem stitch, using black. Sew a small white highlight in each eye.

HAT

With 4 mm (UK 8/US 6) needles and Bright Pink, cast on 40 sts.

Beg with a k row, work 4 rows in st st.

Next row: [P7, k1] 5 times.

Next row: [P1, k7] 5 times.

Rep the last 2 rows 3 times more.

Next row: [P1, [p2tog] 3 times, k1] to end (25 sts).

Next row: [P1, [k2tog] twice] to end (15 sts).

Next row: [P2tog, k1] to end (10 sts).

Next row: [P2tog] to end (5 sts).

Break yarn (leaving a long length for making up), thread through rem 5 sts and draw up tightly.

TO MAKE UP

Using the yarn at the top of the hat, and right sides together, sew seam, reversing the seam for the 4 rows of stocking stitch at the bottom as this will curl back. Make a pom-pom in Blue, approximately 3 cm (1¼ in) in diameter, and attach to top of hat. If desired, stitch hat to top of pig's head.

SCARF

With 4 mm (UK 8/US 6) needles and Bright Pink, cast on 10 sts.

Beg with a k row, and working in st st stripes of 4 rows Bright Pink, 4 rows Blue, 4 rows Green throughout, work until scarf measures 35 cm (14 in) long.

Cast off.

TO MAKE UP

Make two pom-poms in Blue, approximately 3 cm (1¼ in) in diameter. Gather up each end of the scarf and attach a pom-pom to each end. Tie around pig's neck.

Leo Lion

Leo Lion is approximately 33 cm (13 in) tall.

This cheeky little chap, with his fun bright spots and loopy mane is just waiting to be king of your home. The techniques used to create him are relatively easy to do and result in a lovely toy.

MATERIALS
• 2 x 25 g balls of Shetland Wool Brokers 2 ply Jumper Weight in Yellow 23
• 1 x 25 g ball of Shetland Wool Brokers 2 ply Jumper Weight in Gold 91
• 1 x 25 g ball of Shetland Wool Brokers 2 ply Jumper Weight in Purple 20
• 1 x 25 g ball of Shetland Wool Brokers 2 ply Jumper Weight in Orange 73
• 1 x 25 g ball of Shetland Wool Brokers 2 ply Jumper Weight in Royal 18
• 1 x 25 g ball of Shetland Wool Brokers 2 ply Jumper Weight in Red 93
• 1 x 25 g ball of Shetland Wool Brokers 2 ply Jumper Weight in Turquoise 132
• pair of 5.5 mm (UK 5/US 9) knitting needles
• stranded embroidery thread in Black and White
• washable toy stuffing

TENSION
16 sts and 23 rows to 10 cm (4 in) measured over stocking stitch using 5.5 mm (UK 5/US 9) needles and 2 strands of yarn, before hand felting.

Note: Two strands of yarn are used together, throughout, for all pieces.

BODY
RIGHT LEG
* With 5.5 mm (UK 5/US 9) needles and 2 strands of Gold, cast on 10 sts.
Next row: Inc 1 st, k wise, in every st (20 sts).
Beg with a p row, work 5 rows in st st.
Change to Yellow and cont as follows:
Beg with a k row, work 2 rows in st st. *
Row 9: K4 Yellow, k4 Purple, k12 Yellow.
Row 10: P11 Yellow, p6 Purple, p3 Yellow.
Row 11: K3 Yellow, k6 Purple, k11 Yellow.
Row 12: As Row 10.
Row 13: As Row 11.

Row 14: P12 Yellow, p4 Purple, p4 Yellow.
Row 15: K12 Yellow, k4 Orange, k4 Yellow.
Row 16: P3 Yellow, p6 Orange, p11 Yellow.
Row 17: K11 Yellow, k6 Orange, k3 Yellow.
Row 18: As Row 16.
Row 19: As Row 17.
Row 20: P4 Yellow, p4 Orange, p12 Yellow.
Place sts on a spare needle.

LEFT LEG
Work as for right leg from * to *.
Row 9: K4 Yellow, k4 Royal, k12 Yellow.
Row 10: P11 Yellow, p6 Royal, p3 Yellow.
Row 11: K3 Yellow, k6 Royal, k11 Yellow.
Row 12: As Row 10.
Row 13: As Row 11.
Row 14: P12 Yellow, p4 Royal, p4 Yellow.
Row 15: K12 Yellow, k4 Red, k4 Yellow.
Row 16: P3 Yellow, p6 Red, p11 Yellow.
Row 17: K11 Yellow, k6 Red, k3 Yellow.
Row 18: As Row 16.
Row 19: As Row 17.
Row 20: P4 Yellow, p4 Red, p12 Yellow.

JOIN LEGS
With RS facing:
Row 21: K4 Yellow, k4 Orange, k12 Yellow of left leg, then k2 Yellow, k4 Turquoise, k14 Yellow (40 sts).
Row 22: P13 Yellow, p6 Turquoise, p1 Yellow, m1, p11 Yellow, p6 Orange, p3 Yellow (41 sts).
Row 23: K3 Yellow, k6 Orange, k13 Yellow, k6 Turquoise, k13 Yellow.
Row 24: P13 Yellow, p6 Turquoise, p13 Yellow, p6 Orange, p3 Yellow.
Row 25: As Row 23.
Row 26: P14 Yellow, p4 Turquoise, p15 Yellow, p4 Orange, p4 Yellow.
Row 27: K13 Yellow, k4 Purple, k13 Yellow, k4 Royal, k7 Yellow.
Row 28: P6 Yellow, p6 Royal, p11 Yellow, p6 Purple, p12 Yellow.
Row 29: K12 Yellow, k6 Purple, k11 Yellow, k6 Royal, k6 Yellow.
Row 30: As Row 28.
Row 31: As Row 29.
Row 32: P7 Yellow, p4 Royal, p13 Yellow, p4 Purple, p13 Yellow.
Row 33: K5 Yellow, k4 Turquoise, k13 Yellow, k4 Red, k15 Yellow.
Row 34: P14 Yellow, p6 Red, p11 Yellow, p6 Turquoise, p4 Yellow.
Row 35: K4 Yellow, k6 Turquoise, k11 Yellow, k6 Red, k14 Yellow.
Row 36: As Row 34.
Row 37: As Row 35.
Row 38: P15 Yellow, p4 Red, p13 Yellow, p4 Turquoise, p5 Yellow.
Row 39: K14 Yellow, k4 Royal, k14 Yellow, k4 Orange, k5 Yellow.
Row 40: P4 Yellow, p6 Orange, p12 Yellow, p6 Royal, p13 Yellow.
Row 41: K13 Yellow, k6 Royal, k12 Yellow, k6 Orange, k4 Yellow.
Row 42: As Row 40.
Row 43: As Row 41.
Row 44: P5 Yellow, p4 Orange, p14 Yellow, p4 Royal, p14 Yellow.

Row 45: K6 Yellow, k4 Red, k14 Yellow, k4 Purple, k13 Yellow.

Row 46: P12 Yellow, p6 Purple, p12 Yellow, p6 Red, p5 Yellow.

Row 47: K5 Yellow, k6 Red, k12 Yellow, k6 Purple, k12 Yellow.

Row 48: As Row 46.

Row 49: As Row 47.

Row 50: P13 Yellow, p4 Purple, p14 Yellow, p4 Red, p6 Yellow.

Shape shoulders and neck

Cont in Yellow only as follows:

Next row: K9, skpo, k19, k2tog, k9 (39 sts).

P 1 row.

Next row: K2, [k2tog, k1] to last 4 sts, k2tog, k2 (27 sts).

P 1 row.

Next row: K2, [m1, k2] to last st, m1, k1 (40 sts).

Beg with a p row, work 17 rows in st st.

Shape top of head

Next row: K3, [k2tog, k2] to last 5 sts, k2tog, k3 (31 sts).

P 1 row.

Next row: K1, [k2tog] to end (16 sts).

Next row: [P2tog] to end (8 sts).

Cast off.

ARMS

Left arm

With 5.5 mm (UK 5/US 9) needles and 2 ends of Gold, cast on 8 sts.

Next row: Inc 1 st k wise in every st (16 sts).

Beg with a p row, work 5 rows in st st.

Working from Chart A, work 12 rows in st

Shape top

Cont in Yellow only as follows:

Beg with a k row, work 6 rows in st st, dec 1 st at each end of every row (4 sts).

Cast off.

Right arm

Work as for left arm, except work from Chart B.

EARS (make 2)

With 5.5 mm (UK 5/US 9) needles and 2 ends of Yellow, cast on 4 sts.

Beg with a k row, work 2 rows in st st.

** **Next row**: Inc 1 st at each end of row (6 sts).

Beg with a p row, work 3 rows in st st.

Next row: Dec 1 st at each end of row (4 sts).

P 1 row. **

Rep from ** to ** once more.

Cast off.

MANE

With 5.5 mm (UK 5/US 9) needles and 2 ends of Gold, cast on 38 sts.

Next row: K1, [insert needle knitwise into next st, place first two fingers of left hand at back of st, then wind yarn anti-clockwise around needle and fingers twice, draw through the 4 loops] to last st, k1.

Next row: K1, [k2tog, pulling loops down firmly] to last st, k1 (38 sts).

Cast off.

TAIL

With 5.5 mm (UK 5/US 9) needles and 2 ends of Yellow, cast on 3 sts. K 1 row, turn and sl all sts back onto the right needle.

Turn again, and pulling the yarn tight from the left side, k across the 3 sts. In this way you will k all rows and the row ends will pull together to make a tube. Cont in this way until the tail measures 10 cm (4 in).

Cast off.

Cut 6 lengths of Gold, each 6 cm (2¼ in), and loop through one end of the tail using a crochet hook.

FELTING INSTRUCTIONS

Work in all ends with a needle.

Following the instructions in the felting techniques section for hand felting, felt all pieces for approximately 30 minutes.

Reshape while damp, and dry thoroughly.

Chart A

Key
- ☐ Yellow
- ☒ Turquoise
- ⊟ Red

Chart B

Key
- ☐ Yellow
- ☒ Purple
- ⊟ Orange

TO MAKE UP

Join inside leg seams, centre back seam and centre back head seam, leaving an opening halfway up the back. Stuff head firmly. Working with yellow thread and running stitch, sew around neck decreases and increases, draw up tightly and fasten off.

Stuff legs and rest of body and close seam.

Join arm seams, leaving shaped edge open. Stuff and sew to sides of body at shoulders.

Sew ends of mane together to form a circle. Pin to head, stretching slightly, and stitch all around cast-off edge to secure. Stitch again under the knots.

Fold each ear in half and oversew row ends and bottom edges together. Sew to head on top of mane.

Sew end of tail to centre back, just above legs. With black embroidery thread, work eyes and nose in satin stitch. Work stem stitch mouth in black. Sew a small white highlight in each eye.

Chilly Billy

Chilly Billy is approximately 23 cm (9 in) tall.

A happy chap in his hat and scarf; Chilly Billy would make a lovely gift for a toddler or new baby. The stark contrasts of a penguin's colours are known to stimulate new babies' vision.

Materials

• 1 x 50 g ball of Rowan Pure Wool 4-ply, Cashsoft 4-ply or Wool Cotton 4-ply in Black
• 1 x 50 g ball of Rowan Pure Wool 4-ply, Cashsoft 4-ply or Wool Cotton 4-ply in White
• oddments of Orange DK
• small amounts of DK in Red and Pink
• pair 3.25 mm (UK 10/US 3) knitting needles
• stranded embroidery thread in Black and White
• washable toy stuffing

Tension

36 sts and 28 rows to 10 cm (4 in) measured over stocking stitch using 31/4 mm (UK 10/US 3) needles.

BODY AND HEAD

With 3.25 mm (UK 10/US 3) needles and Black, cast on 62 sts.
Beg with a k row, work 2 rows in st st.
Next row: K6, [m1, k10] 5 times, m1, k6 (68 sts).
Beg with a p row, work 27 rows in st st.
SHAPE FOR HEAD
Next row: K6, [k2tog, k16] 3 times, k2tog, k6 (64 sts).
P 1 row.
Next row: K6, [k2tog, k15] 3 times, k2tog, k5 (60 sts).
P 1 row.
Next row: K5, [k2tog, k14] 3 times, k2tog, k5 (56 sts).
P 1 row.
Next row: K6, [k2tog, k12] 3 times, k2tog, k6 (52 sts).
P 1 row.
Next row: K7, [k2tog, k10] 3 times, k2tog, k7

(48 sts).
P 1 row.
Next row: K3, [k2tog, k6] 5 times, k2tog, k3
(42 sts).
Beg with a p row, work 23 rows in st st.
<small>SHAPE TOP OF HEAD</small>
Next row: K3, [k2tog, k3] 7 times, k2tog, k2
(34 sts).
P 1 row.
Next row: K2, [k2tog, k2] 8 times (26 sts).
P 1 row.
Next row: K2, [k2tog, k1] 8 times (18 sts).
P 1 row.
Next row: K1, [k2tog, k1] 5 times, k2tog (12 sts).
Next row: [P2tog] to end (6 sts).
Break yarn (leaving a long length for making up),
thread through remaining 6 sts and draw
up tightly.

BODY BASE

With 3.25 mm (UK 10/US 3) needles and Black,
cast on 10 sts.
Beg with a k row, work 2 rows in st st.
Cast on 2 sts at beg of next 6 rows (22 sts).
Beg with a k row, work 6 rows in st st.
Cast off 2 sts at beg of next 6 rows (10 sts).
Beg with a k row, work 2 rows in st st.
Cast off.

CHEST

With 3.25 mm (UK 10/US 3) needles and White,
cast on 15 sts.
Beg with a k row, work 26 rows in st st.

SHAPE TOP

Next row: K1, skpo, k to last 3 sts, k2tog, k1.
P 1 row.
Rep last 2 rows once more (11 sts).
Next row: K1, skpo, k to last 3 sts, k2tog, k1
(9 sts).
Cast off 2 sts at beg of next 3 rows (3 sts).
Cast off.

WINGS (make 4)

With 3.25 mm (UK 10/US 3) needles and Black,
cast on 7 sts.
Beg with a k row, work 2 rows in st st.
Next row: K1, m1, k to last st, m1, k1.
P 1 row.
Rep the last 2 rows until there are 13 sts.
Beg with a k row, work 14 rows in st st.
Beg with a k row, work 12 rows, dec 1 st at each
end of every foll 4th row (7 sts).
Beg with a k row, work 2 rows in st st.
Cast off 2 sts at beg of next 2 rows (3 sts).
Cast off.

FEET (make 2)

With 3.25 mm (UK 10/US 3) needles and Orange,
cast on 8 sts.
Beg with a k row, work 2 rows in st st.
Beg with a k row, work 5 rows in st st, inc 1 st at
each end of next and every foll k row (14 sts).
Beg with a p row, work 23 rows in st st.
Beg with a k row, work 6 rows in st st, dec 1 st at
each end of next and every foll k row (8 sts).
Cast off.

BEAK

With 3.25 mm (UK 10/US 3) needles and Orange,
cast on 5 sts.
Beg with a k row, work 2 rows in st st.
Next row: Skpo, k1, k2tog (3 sts).
Next row: P2tog, p1 (2 sts).
Next row: K2tog (1 st).
Next row: P, inc into st (2 sts).
Next row: Inc into 1st st, k1 (3 sts).
Next row: Inc into 1st st, p2 (4 sts).
Next row: Inc into 1st st, k3 (5 sts).
P 1 row.
Cast off.

TO MAKE UP

Sew centre back seam of body.
Fold each foot in half and sew down each side.
Stuff lightly and oversew cast-on and cast-off
edges together. Sew two, evenly spaced, lines
through all thicknesses to form toes.
Pin oversewn edges of feet to front lower edge
of body. Pin body base over feet, sew through all
thicknesses, gathering back bottom edge slightly
to fit, and leaving an opening. Stuff firmly and
close opening.
Sew chest to front of body.
Sew two wing pieces together for each wing, and
then sew to sides of body.
Fold beak in half and sew row ends together.
Stitch to face.
Sew eyes in satin stitch using white embroidery
thread. Then sew pupil in each eye with black
thread. Sew a small white highlight in each eye.

SCARF

With 3.25 mm (UK 10/US 3) needles and Pink,
cast on 6 sts and work in g st as follows:
K 2 rows Pink, k 2 rows Red and k 2 rows Orange.
These 6 rows form patt rep. Cont in stripe patt
until scarf measures 30 cm (12 in).
Cast off.

FRINGING

Cut 4 x 8 cm (3 in) lengths each of Pink, Red and
Orange. Following the fringing instructions in the
techniques chapter, knot through each end of the
scarf as per the photograph.

HAT

With 3.25 mm (UK 10/US 3) needles and Pink,
cast on 46 sts.
Beg with a k row, work 16 rows in st st, working
2 rows Pink, 2 rows Red, 2 rows Orange
throughout.
SHAPE TOP
The foll 4 rows are all worked in Orange.
Next row: K1, [k2tog] to last st, k1 (24 sts).
P 1 row.
Next row: [K2tog] to end (12 sts).
Next row: [P2tog] to end (6 sts).
Break yarn (leaving a long length for making up),
thread through remaining 6 sts and draw
up tightly.

TO MAKE UP

Sew centre back seam, reversing the seam for
the last few rows where it curls back. Make a Red
pom-pom and attach to top of hat.

Mice Twice

Mice Twice are approximately 12 cm (4¾ in) tall.

Or even thrice! These mice are an ideal way of using up oddments of wool for a first felting project. Why not knit a few to decorate the desk of a loved one?

MATERIALS
• oddments of Alpaca in Rose, Turquoise and Moss
• pair of 4.5 mm (UK 7/US 7) knitting needles
• stranded embroidery thread in Black and White
• washable toy stuffing

TENSION
20 sts and 26 rows to 10 cm (4 in) measured over stocking stitch using
4.5 mm (UK 7/US 7) needles, before hand felting.

BODY
With 4.5 mm (UK 7/US 7) needles and colour of your choice, cast on 12 sts.
Beg with a k row, work 2 rows in st st.
Next row: [K1, m1] to last st, k1 (23 sts).
P 1 row.
Next row: K8, [m1, k2] 4 times, k7 (27 sts).
P 1 row.
Next row: K9, [m1, k1] 10 times, k8 (37 sts).
Beg with a p row, work 17 rows in st st.
Next row: K8, [k1, k2tog] 7 times, k8 (30 sts).
P 1 row.
Next row: K8, [k2tog] 7 times, k8 (23 sts).
P 1 row.
Beg with a k row, work 10 rows in st st, dec 1 st at each end of every row (3 sts).
Break yarn, thread through rem sts, draw up tightly and fasten off.

EARS (make 2)
With 4.5 mm (UK 7/US 7) needles and colour of your choice, cast on 6 sts.
Beg with a k row, work 4 rows in st st.
Cast off.

FELTING INSTRUCTIONS

Work in all ends with a needle.
Following the instructions for hand felting, felt all pieces for approximately 25 minutes.
NOTE: This yarn will not withstand machine felting.
Reshape while damp, and dry thoroughly.

TO MAKE UP

NOTE: Purl side is right side.
Sew seam along length of body, leaving the cast-on edge open for stuffing. Stuff firmly and close opening.
Sew ears to top of head in line with decreases. Embroider eyes and nose in satin stitch, using black embroidery thread. Sew a small white highlight in each eye.

TAIL

Cut 6 lengths of yarn each 30 cm (12 in) and loop through the bottom of the mouse with a crochet hook. Pull the lengths through until there are equal lengths on each side. Divide the lengths into 3 groups of 4 lengths each and plait to the end. Knot and trim.

Teddy

Teddy is approximately 30 cm (12 in) tall.

Children (and indeed most adults) can never have enough teddies. This little felted fellow is sure to be a great addition to any collection. Why not embroider an initial in the heart on his jumper for a truly individual touch?

MATERIALS
- 1 x 100 g ball of UK Alpaca in Fawn
- oddments of DK yarn in red and yellow
- pair each of 4.5 mm (UK 7/US 7) and 3 mm (UK 11/US 2/3) knitting needles
- stranded embroidery thread in Black and White
- washable toy stuffing

TENSION
UK Alpaca DK
20 sts and 26 rows to 10 cm (4 in) measured over stocking stitch using 41/2 mm (UK 7/US 7) needles, before hand felting.
DK yarn
25 sts and 34 rows to 10 cm (4 in) measured over stocking stitch using 3 mm (UK 11/US 2/3) needles.

BODY FRONT
With 4.5 mm (UK 7/US 7) needles and Fawn, cast on 5 sts.
K 1 row.
Beg with a p row, work 5 rows in st st, at the same time cast on 3 sts at beg of every row (20 sts).
Beg with a k row, work 34 rows in st st.
Cast off 4 sts at beg of next 2 rows (12 sts).
Cast off.

BODY BACK
*With 4.5 mm (UK 7/US 7) needles and Fawn, cast on 2 sts.
Beg with a k row, work 8 rows in st st, at the same time, inc 1 st at each end of Rows 2, 4 and 6 (8 sts). *
Break yarn and place sts on a spare needle.
Make a second piece by rep from * to *.

JOIN PIECES

With RS facing k across 8 sts of second piece, then 8 sts of first piece (16 sts).
Beg with a p row, work 3 rows in st st, inc 1 st at each end of Rows 1 and 3 (20 sts).
Beg with a k row, work 36 rows in st st.
Cast off 4 sts at beg of next 2 rows (12 sts).
Cast off.

HEAD

FRONT

With 4.5 mm (UK 7/US 7) needles and Fawn, cast on 9 sts.
K 1 row.
Next row: P, inc 1 st at each end of row (11 sts).
Next row: K5, m1, k1, m1, k5 (13 sts).
P 1 row.
Next row: K6, m1, k1, m1, k6 (15 sts).
Next row: P, inc 1 st at each end of row (17 sts).
Next row: K8, m1, k1, m1, k8 (19 sts).
P 1 row.
Next row: K9, m1, k1, m1, k9 (21 sts).
Next row: P, inc 1 st at each end of row (23 sts).
Next row: K11, m1, k1, m1, k11 (25 sts).
Beg with a p row, work 3 rows in st st.
Next row: K12, cast off 1 st, k11.
Work on these 12 sts only as follows:
** **Next row**: P to last 2 sts, p2tog.
Next row: Skpo, k to end.
Rep the last 2 rows twice (6 sts).
Now, beg with a p row, work 7 rows in st st, dec 1 st at each end of Rows 3 and 6 (2 sts).
Cast off. **
With WS facing, rejoin yarn to rem 12 sts and work from ** to **, reversing all shapings.

GUSSET

With 4.5 mm (UK 7/US 7) needles and Fawn, cast on 7 sts.
Beg with a k row, work 16 rows in st st, inc 1 st at each end of every 4th row (15 sts).
Beg with a k row, work 10 rows in st st.
Beg with a k row, work 21 rows in st st, dec 1 st at each end of every 3rd row (1 st).
Break yarn and pull through rem st.

ARMS (make 2)

With 4.5 mm (UK 7/US 7) needles and Fawn, cast on 17 sts.
Beg with a k row, work 28 rows in st st.
Next row: K1, [k2tog, k1] to last st, k1 (12 sts).
P 1 row.
Next row: [K2tog] to end (6 sts).
Break yarn, thread through rem sts, and draw up tightly.

LEGS (make 2)

With 4.5 mm (UK 7/US 7) needles and Fawn, cast on 13 sts.

SHAPE FOOT

Row 1: K1, m1, k5, m1, k1, m1, k5, m1, k1 (17 sts).
P 1 row.
Next row: K1, m1, k5, [m1, k1] 6 times, k4, m1, k1 (25 sts).
Next row: P11, [m1, p1] 4 times, p10 (29 sts).
Beg with a k row, work 2 rows in st st.
Next row: K11, [k2tog] 4 times, k10 (25 sts).

P 1 row.
Next row: K9, [k2tog] 4 times, k8. (21 sts.)
Beg with a p row, work 31 rows in st st.
Cast off.

EARS (Make 2)

With 4.5 mm (UK 7/US 7) needles and Fawn, cast
on 6 sts.
Work in moss st throughout, as follows:
Row 1: [K1, p1] to end.
Row 2: [P1, k1] to end.
Incorporating the new sts in to the pattern, inc 1
st at each end of the next row (8 sts).
Work 5 rows in moss st.
Dec 1 st at each end of foll 2 rows (4 sts).
Cast off.

FELTING INSTRUCTIONS

Work in all ends with a needle.
Following the instructions for felting techniques
for hand felting, felt all pieces for approximately
20 minutes.
Reshape while damp, and dry thoroughly.

TO MAKE UP

Sew seam at bottom of back body piece. Sew
sole, heel and centre back seam of each leg.
Stuff, then oversew top edges together. Arrange
tops of legs along slopes at bottom of front body
piece and then arrange back body piece on top.
Sew together through all thicknesses. Sew arm
seams, leaving top open. Stuff and oversew top
edges together. Sew side seams of body to 4 cm
(1½ in) from top. Sew arms into side seams of

body and sew shoulder seams. Stuff body and
close seam. Starting at the bottom edge, sew
gusset to front head. Stuff firmly, moulding as you
go. Sew ears to top of head, placing edge of ear to
gusset seam. Sew head to body. Embroider eyes
and nose in satin stitch, and mouth in stem stitch,
using black. Sew a small white highlight in each
eye.

CLOTHES

JUMPER

Front
* With 3 mm (UK 11/US 2/3) needles and Yellow,
cast on 28 sts.
Beg with a k row, work 2 rows in st st.
Next row: [K2, p2] to end.

Rep the last row once more. *
Change to Red, and beg with a k row, work 6 rows in st st.
Place motif
Next row: K9, k across 9 sts of Row 1 of chart, k10.
Cont working rem 9 rows of chart in st st.
Beg with a k row, work 6 rows in st st.

SHAPE NECK
** **Next row**: K10, cast off 8 sts, k10.
Cont on these 10 sts only as follows:
Next row: P to last 2 sts, p2tog (9 sts).
Next row: Cast off 2 sts, k to end (7 sts).
P 1 row.
Cast off.
With WS facing, rejoin yarn to rem 10 sts and cont as follows:
Next row: Cast off 2 sts, p to end (8 sts).
Next row: K to last 2 sts, k2tog (7 sts).
P 1 row.
Cast off. **

BACK
Work as for front from * to *
Change to Red, and beg with a k row, work 22 rows in st st.
SHAPE NECK
Work as for front from ** to **.

SLEEVES (make 2)
With 3 mm (UK 11/US 2/3) needles and Yellow, cast on 24 sts.
Beg with a k row, work 2 rows in st st.

Next row: [K2, p2] to end.
Rep the last row once more.
Change to Red, and beg with a k row, work 10 rows in st st.
Cast off.

NECK TRIM
Join right shoulder seam.
With RS facing and 3 mm (UK 11/US 2/3) needles and Yellow, pick up and k 3 sts down side front neck, 8 sts across centre front neck, 3 sts up side front neck, 3 sts down side back neck, 8 sts across centre back neck, and 3 sts up side back neck (28 sts).
Next row: [K2, p2] to end.
Rep the last row once more.
Beg with a p row, work 2 rows in st st.
Cast off.

TO MAKE UP
Join left shoulder seam. Arrange the front and back pieces flat and sew sleeves to sides making sure to centre them at the shoulder seams. Sew both under arm and side seams.

Key	
☐	Red
☒	Yellow

CHART

Magic Unicorn

Magic Unicorn is approximately 28 cm (11 in) long.

Unicorns are the stuff of fairytales; just the thing for your little princes and princesses to have endless fun with.

MATERIALS
• 2 x 50 g balls of Sirdar Snuggly Pearls DK in Lilac 430
• 1 x 50 g ball of Sirdar Snuggly Pearls DK in White 251
• small amount of Sirdar Denim Ultra in 502
• pair of 3 mm (UK 11/US 2/3) knitting needles
• stranded embroidery thread in Black and White
• washable toy stuffing

TENSION
26 sts and 38 rows to 10 cm (4 in) measured over stocking stitch using 3 mm (UK 11/US 2/3) needles.

BODY

With 3 mm (UK 11/US 2/3) needles and Lilac, cast on 16 sts.

Beg with a k row, work 2 rows in st st.

Next row: [K1, m1] to last st, k1.

P 1 row.

Rep the last 2 rows once more (61 sts).

Next row: [K15, m1] 3 times, k16 (64 sts).

Beg with a p row, work 71 rows in st st.

Next row: K15, [k2tog, k14] twice, k2tog, k15 (61 sts).

P 1 row.

Next row: K1, [k2tog] to end.

P 1 row.

Rep the last 2 rows once more (16 sts).

Cast off.

LEGS (make 4)

With 3 mm (UK 11/US 2/3) needles and White, cast on 32 sts.

Beg with a k row, work 8 rows in st st.

Change to Lilac, and beg with a k row, work 16 rows in st st.

Beg with a k row, work 6 rows in st st, inc 1 st at each end of the next and foll 2 alt rows (38 sts).

Shape top

Cast off 5 sts at beg of next 2 rows (28 sts).

Cast off 3 sts at beg of next 2 rows (22 sts).

Beg with a k row, work 8 rows in st st, dec 1 st at each end of the next and foll alt rows (14 sts).

Cast off 3 sts at beg of next 4 rows (2 sts).

Cast off.

LEG BASES (make 4)

With 3 mm (UK 11/US 2/3) needles and White, cast on 2 sts.

K 1 row.

Inc 1 st at each end of next 4 rows (10 sts).

Beg with a p row, work 5 rows in st st.

Dec 1 st at each end of next 4 rows (2 sts).

Cast off.

HEAD

With 3 mm (UK 11/US 2/3) needles and Lilac, cast on 58 sts.

Beg with a k row, work 12 rows in st st.

Next row: K4, [k2tog, k5] 7 times, K2tog, k3 (50 sts).

P 1 row.

Next row: K16, [m1, k2] 9 times, m1, k16 (60 sts).

P 1 row.

Next row: K54, turn.

Next row: P48, turn.

Next row: K42, turn.

Next row: P36, turn.

Next row: K35, turn.

Next row: P34, turn.

Next row: K33, turn.

Next row: P32, turn.

Next row: K31, turn.

Next row: P30, turn.

Next row: K29, turn.

Next row: P28, turn.

Next row: K27, turn.

Next row: P26, turn.

Next row: K25, turn.

Next row: P24, turn.

Next row: K23, turn.
Next row: P22, turn.
Next row: K21, turn.
Next row: P20, turn.
Next row: K19, turn.
Next row: P18, turn.
Next row: K17, turn.
Next row: P16, turn.
Next row: K15, turn.
Next row: P14, turn.
Next row: K13, turn.
Next row: P12, turn.
Next row: K11, turn.
Next row: P10, turn.
Next row: K9, turn.
Next row: P8, turn.
Next row: K to end.
Next row: P to end.
Next row: K2, [k2tog, k3] to last 3 sts, k2tog, k1 (48 sts).
P 1 row.
Next row: K14, k2tog, k2, [k2tog, k3] twice, k2tog, k2, k2tog, k14 (43 sts).
P 1 row.
Next row K14, [k2tog, k2] 3 times, k2tog, k15 (39 sts).
P 1 row.
Beg with a k row, work 12 rows in st st.
Next row: K7, skpo, k1, skpo, k15, k2tog, k1, k2tog, k7 (35 sts).
P 1 row.
Next row: K1, [k2tog] to end (18 sts).
Next row: [P2tog] to end (9 sts).
Cast off.

EARS (make 2 Lilac, 2 White)
With 3 mm (UK 11/US 2/3) needles and Lilac, cast on 8 sts.
Beg with a k row, work 8 rows in st st.
P 1 row.
Next row: K14, [k2tog, k2] 3 times, k2tog, k15 (39 sts).
P 1 row.
Beg with a k row, work 12 rows in st st.
Next row: K7, skpo, k1, skpo, k15, k2tog, k1, k2tog, k7 (35 sts).
P 1 row.
Next row: K1, [k2tog] to end (18 sts).
Next row: [P2tog] to end (9 sts).
Cast off.
Dec 1 st at each end of next 3 rows (2 sts).
Cast off.

HORN
With 3 mm (UK 11/US 2/3) needles and White, cast on 20 sts.
Beg with a k row, work 4 rows in st st.
Beg with a k row, work 18 rows in st st, dec 1 st at each end of the next and foll alt rows (2 sts).
Cast off.

TO MAKE UP
Sew one end and underside seam of body.
Stuff firmly.
Tᴀɪʟ: Cut 20 lengths each 15 cm (6 in) of Denim Ultra, and tie a length of yarn around at one end to form a bunch. Place the tied end in the open end of the body piece and close the opening, catching in the bunch of yarn as you go. Join

seam of neck and chin of head piece, then the nose seam. Stuff firmly, then sew to body. Sew each leg seam and then sew a leg base in white end of each leg. Stuff each leg firmly and sew each one to the body.

Sew the long seam of the horn together and stuff. Wrap yarn around horn to form a spiral effect. Sew horn to centre front of head.

Sew one White and one Lilac ear together for each ear and then sew to head each side of horn.

MANE: Cut 16 lengths each 20 cm (8 in) of Denim Ultra and place each piece of yarn on back of head and down neck. Sew through, halfway along each piece, to back of head.

Embroider eyes and nostrils in satin stitch using black embroidery thread. Sew eyelashes in black using straight stitches. Sew mouth in stem stitch in black. Sew a small white highlight in each eye.

Funky Monkey

Funky Monkey is approximately 46 cm (18 in) tall.

> Hide your bananas! The ideal funky fellow to hang around with your own cheeky monkeys. His wonderfully soft fur and extra long scarf set him apart from other monkeys.

MATERIALS

- 2 x 50 g balls of 100 per cent Alpaca DK in Red
- 1 x 50 g ball of 100 per cent Alpaca DK in Orange
- 1 x 50 g ball of 100 per cent Alpaca DK in Indigo
- 1 x 50 g ball of 100 per cent Alpaca DK in Cornflower
- pair each of 4.5 mm (UK 7/US 7) and 4 mm (UK 8/US 6) knitting needles
- stranded embroidery thread in Black and White
- washable toy stuffing

TENSION

20 sts and 25 rows to 10 cm (4 in) measured over stocking stitch using 4.5 mm (UK 7/US 7) needles before machine felting.

BODY

With 4.5 mm (UK 7/US 7) needles and Red, cast on 50 sts.
Beg with a k row, work 2 rows in st st.
Next row: K13, [m1, k1] twice, k21, [m1, k1] twice, k12 (54 sts).
Beg with a p row, work 47 rows in st st.
Next row: K13, [skpo] twice, k20, [k2tog] twice, k13 (50 sts).
P 1 row.
Next row: K10, [skpo] 4 times, k14, [k2tog] 4 times, k10 (42 sts).
P 1 row.
Cast off.

HEAD

With 45 mm (UK 7/US 7) needles and Red, cast on 22 sts.

Beg with a k row, work 2 rows in st st.
Next row: K3, [m1, k4] 4 times, m1, k3 (27 sts).
P 1 row.
Next row: [K3, m1] to last 3 sts, k3 (35 sts).
P 1 row.
Next row: [K2, m1] to last 3 sts, k3 (51 sts).
P 1 row.
Next row: Inc 1 st at each end of row.
P 1 row.
Rep the last 2 rows once more (55 sts).
Beg with a k row, work 16 rows in st st.
Next row: K2, [k2tog, k4] 8 times, k2tog, k3 (46 sts).
P 1 row.
Next row: K2, [k2tog, k3] 8 times, k2tog, k2 (37 sts).
P 1 row.
Next row: K2, [k2tog, k4] 5 times, k2tog, k3 (31 sts).
P 1 row.
Cast off.

FACE

With 4.5 mm (UK 7/US 7) needles and Orange, cast on 13 sts.
Beg with a k row, work 6 rows in st st.
Dec 1 st at each end of foll 2 rows (9 sts).
Cast off.

MUZZLE

With 4.5 mm (UK 7/US 7) needles and Orange, cast on 46 sts.
Beg with a k row, work 8 rows in st st.
Next row: K1, [k2tog, k4] 7 times, k2tog, k1

(38 sts).
P 1 row.
Next row: K1, [k2tog, k3] 7 times, k2tog, k1 (30 sts).
P 1 row.
Next row: [K2tog, k2] 7 times, k2tog (22 sts).
P 1 row.
Cast off.

EARS (make 2 Red, 2 Orange)

With 4.5 mm (UK 7/US 7) needles, cast on 8 sts.
Beg with a k row, work 7 rows in st st.
Dec 1 st at each end of next 3 rows (2 sts).
Cast off.

ARMS (make 2)

With 4.5 mm (UK 7/US 7) needles and Red, cast on 19 sts.

Beg with a k row, work 48 rows in st st.

Cast off.

HANDS (make 2)

With 4.5 mm (UK 7/US 7) needles and Orange, and with the p side of Arm facing, pick up and k 19 sts along cast-off edge.

P 1 row.

Shape thumb

Next row: K9, m1, k1, m1, k9 (21 sts).

P 1 row.

Next row: K9, m1, k3, m1, k9 (23 sts).

P 1 row.

Next row: K1, m1, k8, m1, k5, m1, k8, m1, k1 (27 sts).

P 1 row.

Next row: K1, m1, k9, m1, k7, m1, k9, m1, k1 (31 sts).

P 1 row.

Beg with a k row, work 2 rows in st st.

Next row: K19, turn.

Next row: P8, turn.

Work on these 8 sts only as follows:

Beg with a k row, work 2 rows in st st.

Next row: [K2tog] to end. (5 sts).

Break yarn, thread through rem sts, draw up tightly and fasten off.

SHAPE FOOT

With RS facing, rejoin yarn to rem sts and k across 13 sts of foot, then 14 sts of other side of foot (27 sts).

P 1 row.

Next row: K1, [k2tog] to end (14 sts).

P 1 row.

Next row: [K2tog] to end (7 sts).

Break yarn, thread through rem sts, draw up tightly and fasten off.

TAIL

With 4.5 mm (UK 7/US 7) needles and Red, cast on 8 sts.

K 1 row, turn and sl all sts back onto the right needle.

Turn again, and pulling the yarn tight from the left side, k across the 8 sts. In this way you will k all rows and the row ends will pull together to make a tube.

Cont in this way until the tail measures 22 cm (8½ in).

Break yarn, thread through sts, draw up tightly and fasten off.

FELTING INSTRUCTIONS

Work in all ends with a needle.

Following the instructions for felting techniques for machine felting, felt all pieces in the washing machine on a 60°C wash.

Reshape while damp, and dry thoroughly.

TO MAKE UP

Please note: With the exception of the tail, the purl/reverse side of all Red pieces is the right side. The knit side of all Orange pieces is the right side.

Join each leg, toe and foot seam. Stuff firmly and oversew top edges together.

Sew centre back seam of body.

Place the oversewn ends of the legs at the bottom edge of the body and sew the seam together through all thicknesses.

Stuff the body firmly and oversew the top edge together.

Sew the centre back seam of head. Sew bottom seam, stuff firmly and sew top seam. Sew to body.

Sew ends of muzzle together and then the nose seam. Stuff lightly. Sew face piece to head. Then position muzzle over the bottom edge of the face piece and sew to head.

Sew one Orange and one Red ear together for each ear. Sew to sides of head.

Sew thumb, hand and seam of each arm. Stuff firmly and sew to sides of body.

Sew tail to centre back bottom.

Embroider eyes in satin stitch using black embroidery thread. Sew a small white highlight in each eye. Embroider mouth in stem stitch using black embroidery thread.

SCARF

With 4 mm (UK 8/US 6) needles and Indigo, cast on 105 sts.

Working in g st throughout and 2 rows Indigo, 2 rows Cornflower, work 14 rows.

Cast off.

PLEASE NOTE: Scarf is not felted.

FRINGING: Cut 16 x 10 cm (4 in) lengths of Indigo yarn and 12 x 10 cm (4 in) lengths of Cornflower yarn. Take two lengths and knot through the corresponding coloured stripes at each end of the scarf.

Ellie Flowers

Ellie Flowers is approximately 20 cm (8 in) tall.

A fun, felted, pink elephant, sprinkled in pretty flowers. A charming companion for your little one's trip to the zoo.

MATERIALS
- 2 x 50 g balls of 100 per cent Alpaca DK in Pink
- 1 x 50 g ball of 100 per cent Alpaca DK in Purple
- 1 x 50 g ball of 100 per cent Alpaca DK in Lilac
- 1 x 50 g ball of 100 per cent Alpaca DK in Burgundy
- oddments of Alpaca Select 100% Alpaca DK in Green 22
- pair of 4.5 mm (UK 7/US 7) knitting needles
- stranded embroidery thread in Black
- washable toy stuffing

TENSION
20 sts and 25 rows to 10 cm (4 in) measured over stocking stitch using 4.5 mm (UK 7/US 7) needles before hand felting.

LEFT SIDE BODY
FRONT LEG
* With 4.5 mm (UK 7/US 7) needles and Pink, cast on 10 sts.
K 1 row.
Beg with a p row, work 3 rows in st st, at the same time, inc 1 st at each end of the next 2 rows (14 sts). *
PLACE FLOWER
Next row: K3, k across 9 sts of Row 1 of Chart A, k2.
Beg with a p row, and using the intarsia method, work the rem 11 rows of the chart in st st, inc 1 st at end of final row (15 sts).
Next row: K all sts in Pink.
Next row: P 1 row inc 1 st at end of row (16 sts).
Break yarn and place sts on a spare needle.

BACK LEG

Work as for front leg from * to *.

PLACE FLOWER

Next row: K2, k across 9 sts of Row 1 of Chart B, k3.

Beg with a p row, and using the intarsia method, work the rem 11 rows of the chart in st st, inc 1 st at beg of final row (15 sts).

Next row: K all sts in Pink.

Next row: P 1 row inc 1 st at beg of row (16 sts).

JOIN LEGS

Next row: K across 16 sts of back leg, turn and cast on 4 sts, turn again and with RS facing, k across 16 sts of front leg (36 sts).

P 1 row.

PLACE TWO FLOWERS

Next row: K4, k across 25 sts of Row 1 of Chart C, k7.

Beg with a p row, and using the intarsia method, work 4 rows of the chart in st st.

Next row: Working Row 6 of Chart C, inc 1 st at end of row (37 sts).

Break yarn and place sts on a spare needle.

TAIL

With 4.5 mm (UK 7/US 7) needles and Pink, cast on 3 sts.

Beg with a k row, work 2 rows in st st.

Beg with a k row, work 2 rows in st st, at the same time inc 1 st at end of each row (5 sts).

Beg with a k row, work 2 rows in st st.

Next row: K, inc 1 st at end of row (6 sts).

Beg with a p row, work 3 rows in st st.

Next row: K, inc 1 st at end of row (7 sts).

P 1 row.

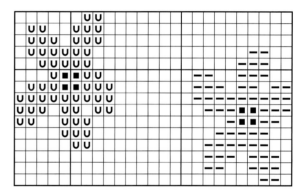

Chart A   Chart B

Chart C

	Key
□	Pink
■	Green
─	Burgundy
▲	Purple
U	Lilac

Chart D

Chart E

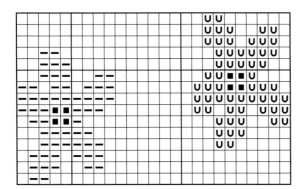

Chart F

JOIN TO BODY

Next row: K across 7 sts of tail, then inc in first st of body and k across rem 36 sts of body (still working the rem rows from Chart C), inc 1 st at end of row (46 sts).

P 1 row.

Break yarn and place sts on a spare needle.

TRUNK

With 4.5 mm (UK 7/US 7) needles and Pink, cast on 3 sts.

K 1 row.

Beg with a p row, work 2 rows in st st, at the same time inc 1 st at each end of both rows (7 sts).

P 1 row.

Next row: K, inc 1 st at end of row (8 sts).

P 1 row.

Next row: K2tog, k to last st, inc 1.

P 1 row.

Next row: K2tog, k to end (7 sts).

P 1 row.

Next row: K to last st, inc 1 (8 sts).

Next row: P to last 2 sts, p2tog (7 sts).

K 1 row.

Next row: Inc 1 st, p to end (8 sts).

Beg with a k row, work 3 rows in st st.

Next row: P to last st, inc 1 (9 sts).

K 1 row.

Next row: P to last st, inc 1 (10 sts).

Next row: Cast on 3 sts, break yarn and place these 13 sts on a spare needle.

JOIN TO BODY

With RS facing, rejoin yarn to body and k across 46 sts of tail and body (still working the rem rows of Chart C), then 13 sts of trunk (59 sts).

Beg with a p row, work 7 rows in st st completing rem rows of Chart C.

PLACE FINAL FLOWER

Next row: K7, k across 9 sts of Row 1 of Chart A, k to last 2 sts, k2tog (58 sts).

Beg with a p row, and using the intarsia method,

work 2 rows of the chart in st st.

Cont to complete Chart A, at the same time dec as follows:

Next row: P to last 2 sts, p2tog.

K 1 row.

Next row: P2tog, p to end.

Beg with a k row, work 2 rows in st st.

Next row: Dec 1 st at each end of row.

P 1 row.

Rep the last 2 rows once more.

Dec 1 st at each end of next 2 rows.

Next row: K2tog, k to end.

Next row: Dec 1 st at each end of row.

Next row: Cast off 2 sts, k to last 2 sts, k2tog.

Next row: P2tog, p to end.

Next row: Cast off 2 sts, k to last 2 sts, k2tog.

Next row: Dec 1 st at each end of row.

Next row: Cast off 5 sts, k to last 2 sts, k2tog.

Next row: Cast off 2 sts, p to end.

Next row: Cast off 5 sts, k to last 2 sts, k2tog.

Next row: Cast off 3 sts, p to end.

Cast off rem 19 sts.

RIGHT SIDE BODY

FRONT LEG

** With 4.5 mm (UK 7/US 7) needles and Pink, cast on 10 sts.

K 1 row.

Beg with a p row, work 3 rows in st st, at the same time, inc 1 st at each end of the next 2 rows (14 sts). **

PLACE FLOWER

Next row: K2, k across 9 sts of Row 1 of Chart D, k3.

Beg with a p row, and using the intarsia method, work the rem 11 rows of the chart in st st, inc 1 st at beg of final row (15 sts).

Next row: K all sts in Pink.

Next row: P 1 row inc 1 st at beg of row (16 sts).

Break yarn and place sts on a spare needle.

BACK LEG

Work as for front leg from ** to **.

PLACE FLOWER

Next row: K3, k across 9 sts of Row 1 of Chart E, k2.

Beg with a p row, and using the intarsia method, work the rem 11 rows of the chart in st st, inc 1 st at end of final row (15 sts).

Next row: K all sts in Pink.

Next row: P 1 row inc 1 st at end of row (16 sts).

Turn and cast on 4 sts (20 sts).

Break yarn and place sts on a spare needle.

JOIN LEGS

Next row: With RS facing and Pink, k across 16 sts of front leg, and k across 20 sts of back leg. (36 sts).

P 1 row.

PLACE TWO FLOWERS

Next row: K7, k across 25 sts of Row 1 of Chart F, k4.

Beg with a p row, and using the intarsia method, work 4 rows of the chart in st st.

Next row: Working Row 6 of Chart F, inc 1 st at beg of row (37 sts).

Break yarn and place sts on a spare needle.

Next row: Inc in the first st, k across 37 sts of body (still working the rem rows from Chart F), then inc in first st of tail and k rem 6 sts of tail (46 sts).
P 1 row.
Break yarn and place sts on a spare needle.

TRUNK

With 4.5 mm (UK 7/US 7) needles and Pink, cast on 3 sts.
K 1 row.
Beg with a p row, work 2 rows in st st, at the same time inc 1 st at each end of both rows (7 sts).
P 1 row.
Next row: K, inc 1 st at beg of row (8 sts).
P 1 row.
Next row: Inc 1, k to last 2 sts, k2tog.
P 1 row.
Next row: K to last 2 sts, k2tog (7 sts).
P 1 row.
Next row: Inc 1, k to end (8 sts).
Next row: P2tog, p to end (7 sts).
K 1 row.
Next row: P to last st, inc 1 (8 sts).
Beg with a k row, work 3 rows in st st.
Next row: Inc 1, p to end (9 sts).
K 1 row.
Next row: Inc 1, p to end (10 sts).
JOIN TO BODY
With RS facing, k across 10 sts of trunk, turn and cast on 3 sts, turn again and k across 46 sts of

TAIL

With 4.5 mm (UK 7/US 7) needles and Pink, cast on 3 sts.
Beg with a k row, work 2 rows in st st.
Beg with a k row, work 2 rows in st st, at the same time inc 1 st at beg of both rows (5 sts).
Beg with a k row, work 2 rows in st st.
Next row: K, inc 1 st at beg of row (6 sts).
Beg with a p row, work 3 rows in st st.
Next row: K, inc 1 st at beg of row (7 sts).
P 1 row.

body and tail (still working the rem rows of Chart F) (59 sts).

Beg with a p row, work 7 rows in st st completing rem rows of Chart F.

Place Final Flower

Next row: K2tog, k41, k across 9 sts of Row 1 of Chart D, k7.

Beg with a p row, and using the intarsia method, work 2 rows of the chart in st st.

Cont to complete Chart D, at the same time dec as follows.

Next row: P2tog, p to end.

K 1 row.

Next row: P to last 2 sts, p2tog.

Beg with a k row, work 2 rows in st st.

Next row: Dec 1 st at each end of row.

P 1 row.

Rep the last 2 rows once more.

Dec 1 st at each end of next 2 rows.

Next row: K to last 2 sts, k2tog.

Next row: Dec 1 st at each end of row.

Next row: K2tog, k to end.

Next row: Cast off 2 sts, p to last 2 sts, p2tog.

Next row: K2tog, k to end.

Next row: Cast off 2 sts, p to last 2 sts, p2tog

Next row: K2tog, k to end.

Next row: Cast off 5 sts, p to last 2 sts, p2tog.

Next row: Cast off 2 sts, k to end.

Next row: Cast off 5 sts, p to last 2 sts, p2tog.

Next row: Cast off 3 sts, k to end.

Cast off rem 19 sts.

GUSSET

Front leg

*** With 4.5 mm (UK 7/US 7) needles and Pink, cast on 10 sts.

K 1 row.

Beg with a p row, work 2 rows in st st, at the same time, inc 1 st at each end of both rows (14 sts).

Beg with a p row, work 12 rows in st st. ***

Next row: P, inc 1 st at beg of row.

K 1 row.

Next row: P, inc 1 st at beg of row (16 sts).

Break yarn and place sts on a spare needle.

Back leg

Work as for front leg from *** to ***.

Next row: P, inc 1 st at end of row.

K 1 row.

Next row: P, inc 1 st at end of row (16 sts).

Turn and cast on 4 sts (20 sts).

Break yarn and place sts on a spare needle.

Join legs

With RS facing and Pink, k across 16 sts of front leg and 20 sts of back leg (36 sts).

Beg with a p row, work 5 rows in st st, at the same time, inc 1 st at each end of every row (46 sts).

K 1 row.

Beg with a p row, work 5 rows in st st, at the same time, dec 1 st at each end of every row (36 sts).

Divide for legs

Next row: K16, turn.

Work on these 16 sts only as follows:

Next row: P2tog, p to end.

K 1 row.
Next row: P2tog, p to end (14 sts).
**** Beg with a k row, work 12 rows in st st.
Dec 1 st at each end of the next 2 rows (10 sts).
Cast off. ****
With RS facing and Pink, rejoin yarn to rem sts
and work as follows:
Next row: Cast off 4 sts, k to end (16 sts).
Next row: P to last 2 sts, p2tog.
K 1 row.
Next row: P to last 2 sts, p2tog.
Work as for first leg from **** to ****.

EARS (make 2)
With 4.5 mm (UK 7/US 7) needles and Pink, cast
on 11 sts.
Beg with a k row, work 2 rows in st st.
Next row: Inc 1 st at each end of row.
P 1 row.
Rep the last 2 rows, twice more (17 sts).
Next row: Dec 1 st at each end of row.
P 1 row.
Rep the last 2 rows, once more (13 sts).
Cast off.

SADDLE
With 4.5 mm (UK 7/US 7) needles and Lilac, cast
on 5 sts.
K 2 rows.
Next row: K2, m1, k to last 2 sts, m1, k2.
Next row: K2, p to last 2 sts, k2.
Keeping the 2 sts at either edge in g st on every
row, work stripes of 2 rows Pink, 2 rows Green,
4 rows Lilac, and inc on every 3rd row to 15 sts.

Then inc 1 st at each end of every alt row to
19 sts.
Work 4 rows in st st, still keeping the edges in
g st.
Next row: K2, k2tog, k to last 4 sts, k2tog, k2.
Next row: K2, p to last 2 sts, k2.
Rep the last 2 rows once more.
Then dec at each end of every 3rd row until 5 sts
rem.
K 2 rows.
Cast off.

FELTING INSTRUCTIONS
Work in all ends with a needle.
Following the instructions for hand felting, felt all
pieces for approximately 30 minutes.
Reshape while damp, and dry thoroughly.

TO MAKE UP
With right sides together, sew the gusset to the
corresponding legs, and the points along the
edges under the tail and trunk.
Sew left and right side pieces together, curving
the seam to follow the shaping and leaving an
opening at the top of the back.
Turn right side out and push out all seams. Stuff
firmly and close opening.
Attach ears at each side of head, and stitch
saddle to back.
Embroider eyes on each side of head using black
embroidery thread and satin stitch.

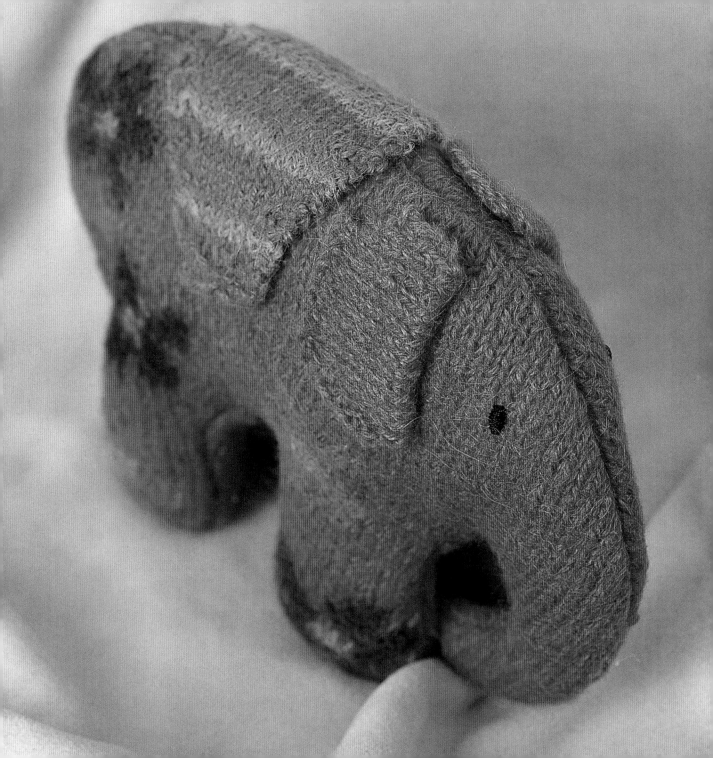

Fluffy Puppy

Fluffy Puppy is approximately 25 cm (10 in) long.

Everyone's best friend; Fluffy Puppy could be a first pet for a child. His intarsia spots add to his cuteness and he is the perfect size to tuck under a child's arm.

MATERIALS

• 2 x 50 g balls of 100 per cent Alpaca DK in Cream
• 1 x 50 g ball of100 per cent Alpaca DK in Brown
• 1 x 50 g ball of 100 per cent Alpaca DK in Tan
• oddments of 100 per cent Alpaca DK in Red
• pair each of 4.5 mm (UK 7/US 7) and 4 mm (UK8/US 6) knitting needles
• stranded embroidery thread in Black and White
• washable toy stuffing

TENSION

20 sts and 25 rows to 10 cm (4 in) measured over stocking stitch using 4.5 mm (UK 7/US 7) needles before machine felting.

LEFT SIDE BODY

FRONT LEG

With 4.5 mm (UK 7/US 7) needles and Cream, cast on 14 sts.
Beg with a k row, work 8 rows in st st.
Using the intarsia method, cont as follows:
Row 9: K12 Cream, k2 Brown.
Row 10: P4 Brown, p10 Cream.
Row 11: K8 Cream, k6 Brown.
Row 12: P7 Brown, p7 Cream.
Row 13: K6 Cream, k8 Brown.
Row 14: P8 Brown, p6 Cream .
Row 15: As Row 13.
Row 16: P9 Brown, p5 Cream.
Break yarn and place sts on a spare needle.

Back leg

With 4.5 mm (UK 7/US 7) needles and Cream, cast on 14 sts.

Beg with a k row, work 4 rows in st st.

Row 5: K6 Cream, k4 Brown, k4 Cream.
Row 6: P3 Cream, p6 Brown, p5 Cream.
Row 7: K4 Cream, k8 Brown, k2 Cream.
Row 8: P2 Cream, p8 Brown, p4 Cream.
Row 9: As Row 7.
Row 10: As Row 8.
Row 11: K5 Cream, k7 Brown, k2 Cream.
Row 12: P2 Cream, p7 Brown, p5 Cream.
Row 13: K6 Cream, k5 Brown, k3 Cream.
Row 14: P5 Cream, p2 Brown, p7 Cream.
Row 15: K3 Tan, k11 Cream.
Row 16: Cast on 12 sts, p22 Cream, p4 Tan.

Join legs

Row 17: With RS facing, k5 Tan, k21 Cream of back leg, then k5 Cream, k9 Brown of front leg (40 sts).
Row 18: P9 Brown, p25 Cream, p6 Tan.
Row 19: K6 Tan, k25 Cream, k9 Brown.
Row 20: P8 Brown, p26 Cream, p6 Tan.
Row 21: K6 Tan, k17 Cream, k4 Tan, k5 Cream, k8 Brown.
Row 22: P7 Brown, p5 Cream, p6 Tan, p15 Cream, p7 Tan.
Row 23: K7 Tan, k15 Cream, k6 Tan, k6 Cream, k6 Brown.
Row 24: P5 Brown, p6 Cream, p8 Tan, p14 Cream, p7 Tan.
Row 25: K7 Tan, k14 Cream, k8 Tan, k7 Cream, k4 Brown.
Row 26: P3 Brown, p8 Cream, p8 Tan, p14 Cream, p7 Tan.
Row 27: K6 Tan, k15 Cream, k8 Tan, k11 Cream.
Row 28: P11 Cream, p7 Tan, p16 Cream, p6 Tan.
Row 29: K6 Tan, k17 Cream, k5 Tan, k12 Cream.
Row 30: Cast on 15 sts, p28 Cream, p3 Tan, p19 Cream, p5 Tan (55 sts).
Row 31: K4 Tan, k9 Cream, k5 Brown, k37 Cream.
Row 32: P35 Cream, p9 Brown, p8 Cream, p3 Tan.
Row 33: K10 Cream, k12 Brown, k33 Cream.
Row 34: P32 Cream, p14 Brown, p9 Cream.
Row 35: K8 Cream, k16 Brown, k31 Cream.
Row 36: P30 Cream, p17 Brown, p8 Cream.
Row 37: K7 Cream, k18 Brown, k6 Cream, k6 Tan, k18 Cream.
Row 38: P17 Cream, p8 Tan, p5 Cream, p18 Brown, p7 Cream.
Row 39: K7 Cream, k19 Brown, k3 Cream, k10 Tan, k16 Cream.
Row 40: P16 Cream, p10 Tan, p3 Cream, p19 Brown, p7 Cream.
Row 41: K6 Cream, cast off 25 sts, k9 Tan, k15 Cream.

Working on these 24 sts of head only, cont as follows:

Row 42: P15 Cream, p9 Tan.
Row 43: K2tog Tan, k7 Tan, k15 Cream.
Row 44: P15 Cream, p8 Tan.
Row 45: K2tog Tan, k6 Tan, k13 Cream, k2tog Cream.
Row 46: Cast off 2 sts, p12 Cream, p7 Tan.
Row 47: K2tog Tan, K5 Tan, k12 Cream.
Row 48: Cast off 4 sts, p9 Cream, p5 Tan.
Row 49: K2tog Tan, k2 Tan, k10 Cream.
Row 50: Cast off 5 sts, p6 Cream, p2 Tan.

Row 51: K8 Cream.
Row 52: Cast off 3 sts, p5 Cream.
Row 53: K3, k2tog.
Row 54: P2tog, p2 (3 sts).
Beg with a k row, work 2 rows in st st.
Cast off.
With WS facing, rejoin yarn to rem 6 sts for tail and cont as follows:
Beg with p row, work 15 rows, dec 1 st at inside edge of every 5th row (3 sts).
Cast off.

RIGHT SIDE BODY

FRONT LEG

With 4.5 mm (UK 7/US 7) needles and Cream, cast on 14 sts.
Beg with a k row, work 8 rows in st st.
Using the intarsia method, cont as follows:
Row 9: K2 Brown, k12 Cream.
Row 10: P10 Cream, p4 Brown.
Row 11: K6 Brown, k8 Cream.
Row 12: P7 Cream, p7 Brown.
Row 13: K8 Brown, k6 Cream.
Row 14: P6 Cream, p8 Brown.
Row 15: As Row 13.
Row 16: P5 Cream, p9 Brown.
Break yarn and place sts on a spare needle.

BACK LEG

With 4.5 mm (UK 7/US 7) needles and Cream, cast on 14 sts.
Beg with a k row, work 4 rows in st st.
Row 5: K4 Cream, k4 Brown, k6 Cream.
Row 6: P5 Cream, p6 Brown, p3 Cream.

Row 7: K2 Cream, k8 Brown, k4 Cream.

Row 8: P4 Cream, p8 Brown, p2 Cream.

Row 9: As Row 7.

Row 10: As Row 8.

Row 11: K2 Cream, k7 Brown, k5 Cream.

Row 12: P5 Cream, p7 Brown, p2 Cream.

Row 13: K3 Cream, k5 Brown, k6 Cream.

Row 14: P7 Cream, p2 Brown, p5 Cream.

Row 15: K11 Cream, k3 Tan.

Row 16: P4 Tan, p10 Cream.

Turn and cast on 12 sts.

JOIN LEGS

Row 17: With RS facing, k9 Brown, k5 Cream of front leg, then k21 Cream, k5 Tan, of back leg (40 sts).

Row 18: P6 Tan, p25 Cream, p9 Brown.

Row 19: K9 Brown, k25 Cream, k6 Tan.

Row 20: P6 Tan, p26 Cream, p8 Brown.

Row 21: K8 Brown, k5 Cream, k4 Tan, k17 Cream, k6 Tan.

Row 22: P7 Tan, p15 Cream, p6 Tan, p5 Cream, p7 Brown.

Row 23: K6 Brown, k6 Cream, k6 Tan, k15 Cream, k7 Tan.

Row 24: P7 Tan, p14 Cream, p8 Tan, p6 Cream, p5 Brown.

Row 25: K4 Brown, k7 Cream, K8 Tan, k14 Cream, k7 Tan.

Row 26: P7 Tan, p14 Cream, p8 Tan, p8 Cream, p3 Brown.

Row 27: K11 Cream, k8 Tan, k15 Cream, k6 Tan.

Row 28: P6 Tan, p16 Cream, p7 Tan, p11 Cream.

Row 29: K12 Cream, k5 Tan, k17 Cream, k6 Tan.

Row 30: P5 Tan, p19 Cream, p3 Tan, p13 Cream.

Row 31: Cast on 15 sts, k37 Cream, k5 Brown, k9 Cream, k4 Tan (55 sts).

Row 32: P3 Tan, p8 Cream, p9 Brown, p35 Cream.

Row 33: K33 Cream, k12 Brown, k10 Cream.

Row 34: P9 Cream, p14 Brown, p32 Cream.

Row 35: K31 Cream, k16 Brown, k8 Cream.

Row 36: P8 Cream, p17 Brown, p30 Cream.

Row 37: K18 Cream, k6 Tan, k6 Cream, k18 Brown, k7 Cream.

Row 38: P7 Cream, p18 Brown, p5 Cream, p8 Tan, p17 Cream.

Row 39: K16 Cream, k10 Tan, k3 Cream, k19 Brown, k7 Cream.

Row 40: P7 Cream, p19 Brown, p3 Cream, p10 Tan, p16 Cream.

Row 41: K15 Cream, k9 Tan, cast off 25 sts, k6 Cream.

Working on these 6 sts of tail only, cont as follows:

Beg with p row, work 15 rows, dec 1 st at inside edge of every 5th row (3 sts).

Cast off.

With WS facing, rejoin yarn to rem 24 sts for head and cont as follows:

Row 42: P9 Tan, p15 Cream.

Row 43: K15 Cream, k7 Tan, k2tog (23 sts).

Row 44: P8 Tan, p15 Cream.

Row 45: K2tog Cream, k13 Cream, k6 Tan, k2tog.

Row 46: P7 Tan, p14 Cream.

Row 47: Cast off 2 sts, k12 Cream, k5 Tan, k2tog.

Row 48: P5 Tan, p13 Cream.

Row 49: Cast off 4 sts, k10 Cream, k2 Tan, k2tog.

Row 50: P2 Tan, p11 Cream.

Row 51: Cast off 5 sts, k8 Cream.

Row 52: P8 Cream.
Row 53: Cast off 3 sts, k5.
Row 54: P5.
Row 55: Cast off 2 sts, k3.
Row 56: P3.
Cast off.

BODY GUSSET

With 4.5 mm (UK 7/US 7) needles and Cream,
cast on 2 sts.
Beg with a k row, work 6 rows in st st, inc 1 st at
each end of every alt row (8 sts).
Beg with a k row, work 24 rows in st st.
Cast on 14 sts at beg of next 2 rows (36 sts).
Beg with a k row, work 16 rows in st st.
Cast off 12 sts at beg of next 2 rows (12 sts).
Beg with a k row, work 14 rows in st st.
Cast on 12 sts at beg of next 2 rows (36 sts).
Beg with a k row, work 16 rows in st st.
Cast off 15 sts at beg of next 2 rows (6 sts).
Beg with a k row, work 6 rows in st st, dec 1 st at
each end of every 3rd row (2 sts).
Cast off.

HEAD GUSSET

With 4.5 mm (UK 7/US 7) needles and Cream,
cast on 2 sts.
Beg with a k row, work 8 rows in st st, inc 1 st at
each end of every 4th row (6 sts).
Beg with a k row, work 16 rows in st st.
Beg with a k row, work 3 rows in st st, inc 1 st at
each end of every row (12 sts).
P1 row.
K 1 row.

Beg with a p row, work 3 rows in st st, dec 1 st at
each end of every row (6 sts).
Beg with a k row, work 8 rows in st st, dec 1 st at
each end of every foll 3rd row (2 sts).
Cast off.

FELTING INSTRUCTIONS

Work in all ends with a needle.
Following the instructions for felting techniques
for machine felting, felt all pieces in the washing
machine on a 60°C wash.
Reshape while damp, and dry thoroughly.

TO MAKE UP

Stitch head gusset between ears on each
head piece, sewing the long end down towards
the nose.
Sew centre back seam of body pieces.
Sew body gusset to legs and lower body,
leaving the tail end open for stuffing. Stuff firmly
and close opening.
Embroider eyes and nose in satin stitch, using
black embroidery thread. Embroider mouth in
stem stitch using black embroidery thread. Sew a
small white highlight in each eye.

COLLAR

With 4 mm (UK 8/US 6) needles and Red, cast on
30 sts.
K 2 rows.
Cast off.
Wrap collar around neck of dog and join ends.

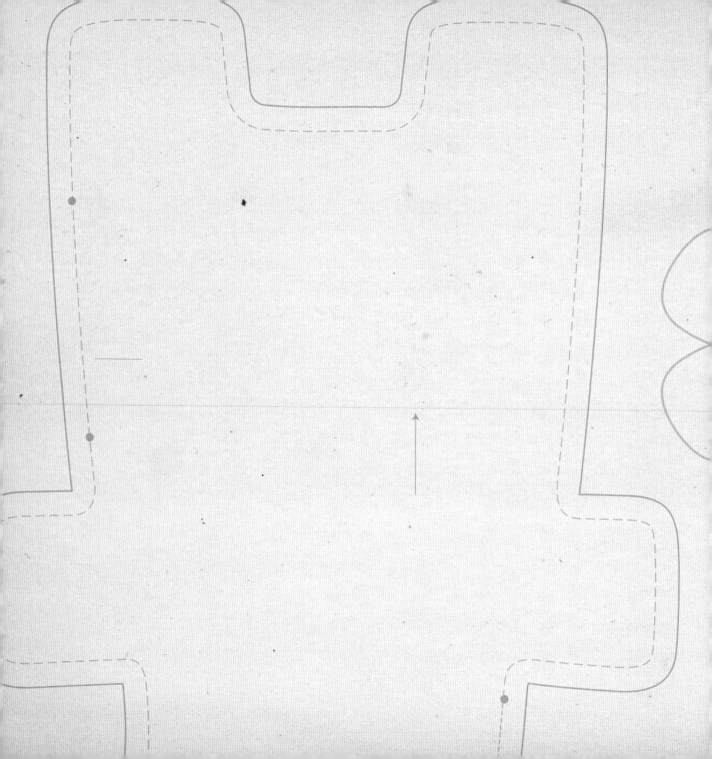

Templates

All templates are shown at
75 per cent of actual size

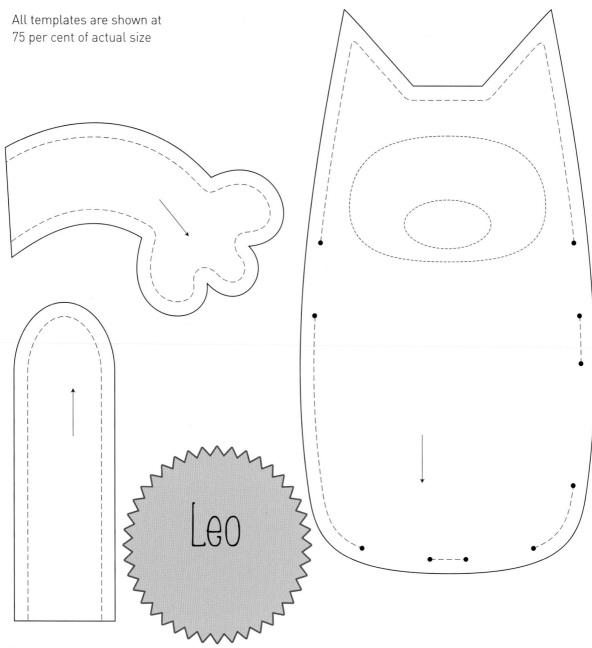

Leo

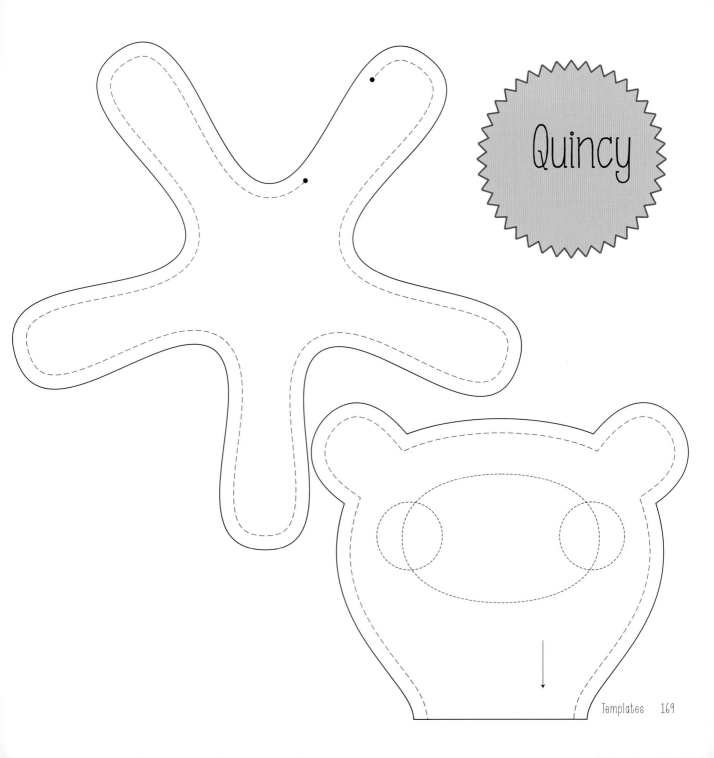

Quincy

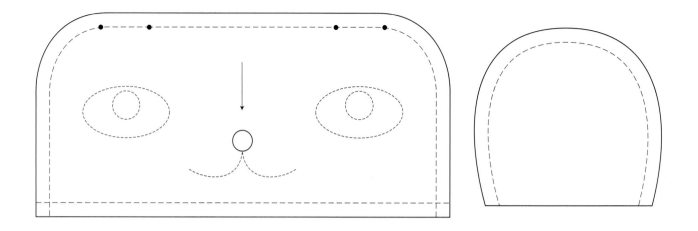

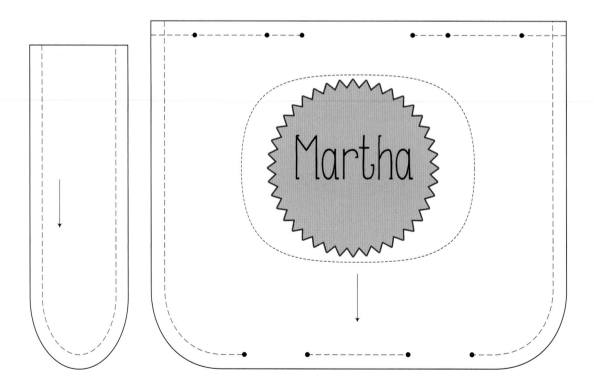

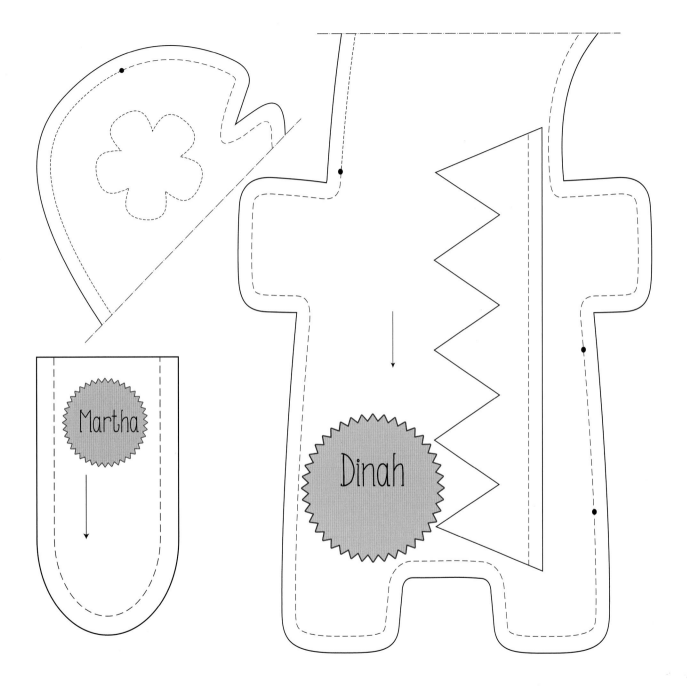

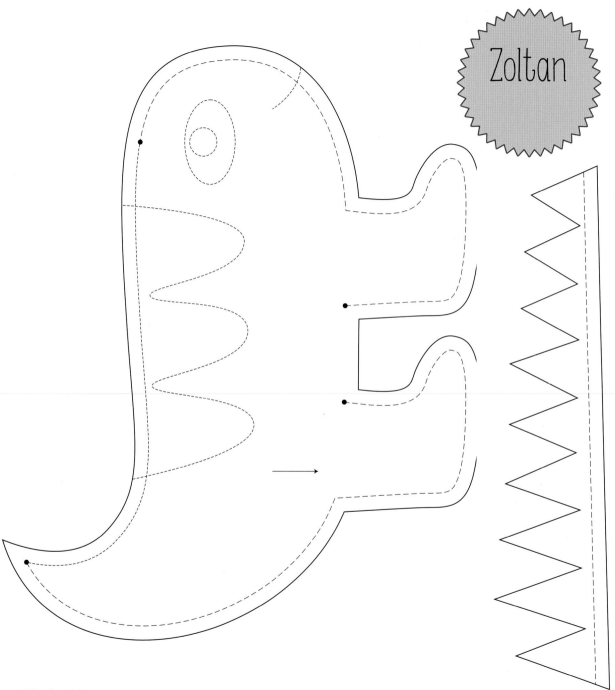

Zoltan

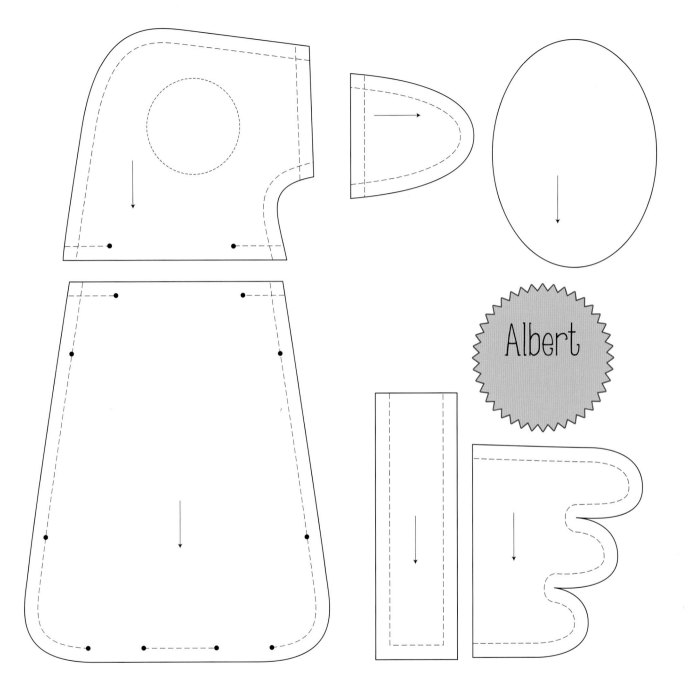

Albert

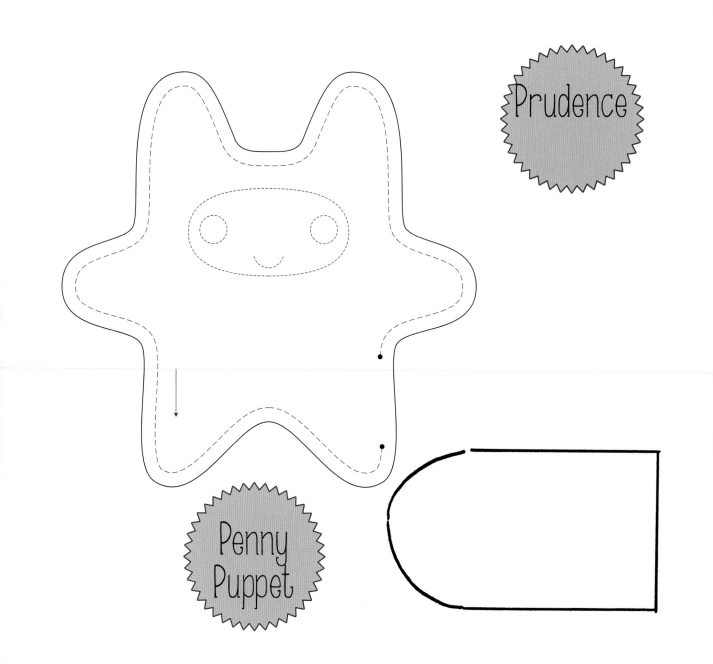

Prudence

Penny
Puppet

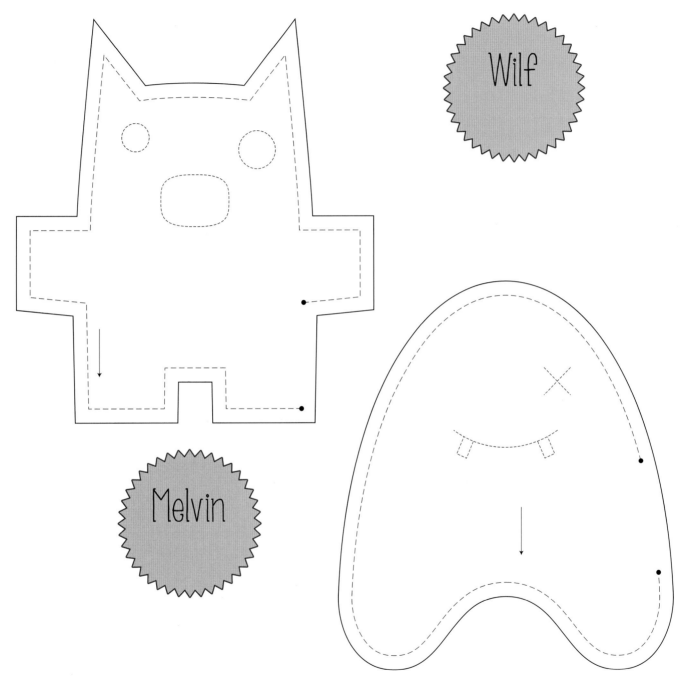

Wilf

Melvin

Index